Scaffolding Student Learning

*Other volumes in the **Advances in Learning & Teaching** Series*
Steve Graham, Karen R. Harris, & Michael Pressley, Series Editors

Teaching Every Child Every Day:
Learning in Diverse Schools and Classrooms
Karen R. Harris, Steve Graham, Don Deshler, & Michael Pressley, Editors
(1997)

Scaffolding Student Learning

Instructional Approaches and Issues

Kathleen Hogan

Michael Pressley

The University at Albany, State University of New York

EDITORS

BROOK
LINE
BOOKS

ISBN 1-57129-036-2

Library of Congress Cataloging-In-Publication Data
Scaffolding student learning: instructional approaches and issues /
    Kathleen Hogan, Michael Pressley, editors.
        p.   cm.
    Includes bibliographical references and index.
    ISBN 1-57129-036-2 (pbk.)
        1. Teaching.   2. Learning.   3. Constructivism (Education).
4. Tutors and tutoring.   I. Hogan, Kathleen.   II. Pressley,
Michael.
LB1027.S289   1997
371.39--dc21

Printed in Canada by Best Book Manufacturing, Louiseville, Quebec.

Published by
BROOKLINE BOOKS
P.O. Box 1047
Cambridge, Massachusetts 02238
Order toll-free: 1-800-666-BOOK

CONTENTS

Introduction 1
Kathleen Hogan

Chapter 1
Scaffolding: A Powerful Tool in Social Constructivist
Classrooms 6
Laura R. Roehler & Danise J. Cantlon

Chapter 2
Scaffolding the Development of Intelligence among
Children who are Delayed in Learning to Read 43
Irene W. Gaskins, Sharon Rauch, Eleanor Gensemer, Elizabeth
Cunicelli, Colleen O'Hara, Linda Six, & Theresa Scott

Chapter 3
Scaffolding Scientific Competencies within Classroom
Communities of Inquiry 74
Kathleen Hogan & Michael Pressley

Chapter 4
Scaffolding Techniques of Expert Human Tutors 108
Mark R. Lepper, Michael F. Drake, & Theresa O'Donnell-Johnson

Chapter 5
An Anatomy of Naturalistic Tutoring 145
Arthur C. Graesser, Cheryl Bowers, Douglas J. Hacker,
& Natalie Person

Afterword
Becoming a Scaffolder of Students' Learning................... 185
Kathleen Hogan & Michael Pressley

Index 192

SERIES FOREWORD

This is the initial volume in the continuing series Advances in Learning and Teaching. Steve Graham, Karen Harris, and Michael Pressley are the general editors of the series, which will focus on important contemporary topics relevant to school-based achievement and pedagogy. The general editors' goal at the outset of the series is to publish between one and three volumes a year.

Each volume in the series will focus on a single topic, bringing together commentary from some of the most important figures contributing to the problem area. The plan at this time is for at least one of the general editors to be involved in the editing of each volume, although often in collaboration with guest editors who are exceptionally expert with respect to the topic of the volume. Those interested in serving as guest editors should contact one of the general editors with a specific proposal for a volume.

Introduction

KATHLEEN HOGAN, The University at Albany,
State University of New York

In recent years there has been an upsurge of interest in forms of instruction that capitalize on the social nature of classrooms. Researchers and practitioners are examining how the social context of learning influences such important processes as constructivemeaning-making and self-regulation of learning. In fact, many characterize all higher-order thinking as dialogical, meaning that more sophisticated thinking entails having an imagined conversation about your ideas. This type of thinking becomes possible through internalizing actual experiences of thinking aloud with another person.

A crucial aspect of learning through social interaction is *dialogue*. How members of an intellectual community talk with one another constitutes in large measure the practice of their discipline. So teachers who want to give their students authentic experiences in the disciplines they study in school help them talk like scientists or writers or historians. Students become socialized into the talk and practices of different disciplines through interaction with more skilled members of the discipline — i.e., their teacher.

Instructional scaffolding lies at the heart of the verbal interactions that induct students into the practices of an academic discipline. Therefore, the researchers' and practitioners' insights collected in this volume should appeal to all those who are interested in social forms of instruction, in promoting sophisticated thinking abilities in students, and in preparing students for workplaces where intellectual teamwork is the norm.

In addition to being a tool for enculturating students into the thinking patterns of experts, instructional scaffolding is an effective way to help students accomplish discrete learning tasks. A teacher who stops by a student's desk to ask questions to determine her progress, and then provides hints, subtle suggestions, and guidance to move the student along, is using instructional scaffolding. Scaffolding means providing support to allow a child to think for him or herself. The more advanced partner, or scaffolder, is supportive without being overly directive. A good scaffolder looks for the point where a student can go it alone, and allows the individual to proceed on his or her own initiative.

Scaffolding is a challenging form of instruction, but as the chapters in this volume suggest, it can be done successfully both in classroom and one-to-one settings. A teacher who scaffolds a whole class of students has to deal not only with the complexity of each individual student's cognition, but of having a whole group of students who are at varying places in their learning. Students differ from one another in how much scaffolding they need, and an individual student's need for assistance differs from task to task.

The chapters in this volume illustrate how competent scaffolders manage complexities such as these. Taken as a whole, the chapters cover a wide range of territory, including diverse goals of scaffolding (teaching specific knowledge and skills, building general intellectual habits, and fostering motivational and affective outcomes), settings (one-to-one, small group, and whole class), styles (direct instruction and engagement in learning conversations), content areas (math, science, and language arts), and student populations (elementary, middle school, high school, and college students; delayed and normal learners). The levels of analysis also differ among chapters, with some providing information about scaffolding at the micro level of discourse moves, while others analyze scaffolding conversations more holistically. Together the chapters present a well-rounded portrayal of the many manifestations of scaffolding.

Roehler and Cantlon contribute the first chapter, entitled "Scaffolding: A Powerful Tool in Social Constructivist Classrooms." They analyze two elementary classrooms where the teachers follow the literacy cycle, during which students progress from guided reading and writing, to creating drafts of original writing, to editing their work into a final draft, and then present their final products. The authors delineate several types of scaffolding that occur during learning conversations in these classrooms: teachers offer explanations, invite student participation, verify and clarify student understandings, and model desired behaviors. They then portray scaffolding over time within a language arts unit on "tall tales." Several principles of scaffolding emerged through their analysis, including the delicate balance between challenging and supporting students, temporary and permanent forms of scaffolding, and the role of modeling dispositions and character traits, such as respect for evidence, tentativeness, willingness to suspend decisions, and openness to competing ideas.

In Chapter 2, "Scaffolding the Development of Intelligence Among Children Who are Delayed in Learning to Read," Gaskins, Rauch, Gensemer, Cunicelli, O'Hara, Six, and Scott provide many examples of scaffolding with excerpts from lessons at the Benchmark School. The teachers at Benchmark use scaffolding as a tool for providing instruction in strategies for intelligent thinking and behavior. The chapter illustrates how these teachers use scaffolding to teach content knowledge, strategies, and dispositions. The examples of content instruction are from a first-grade mathematics class that is learning to recognize and build patterns, and from a middle-school language arts class aimed at heightening students' realization that content knowledge plays a role in interpreting text. Examples of using scaffolding for strategies instruction come from a third-grade class on decoding multisyllabic words, and a middle-school science class in which students are searching texts and taking notes to develop an understanding of the vocabulary tied to their topic of research. Finally, the authors illustrate how to guide the development of dispositions through scaffolding with second- and third-graders learning to identify the dispositional elements of intelligent mathematical behavior, and with middle-school students learning to articulate their personal style and how to control it when it is a barrier to learning.

Hogan and Pressley focus on whole-class scaffolding in Chapter 3, "Scaffolding Scientific Competencies within Classroom Communities of Inquiry." They analyze the talk in middle and high school inquiry-based science classrooms where students work on authentic problems that require them to build explanations and models from evidence. The teachers in these classrooms think together with students in whole-class discussions aimed at immersing students in the practices and standards of scientific discourse. During these discussions, the teachers do not evaluate students' ideas, but rather encourage them to explore and develop their thoughts aloud. Excerpts of classroom dialogue are analyzed to point out the types of statements and subtle cues that teachers use to prompt student thinking. The chapter also presents some student perspectives on scaffolding, tips on how to begin scaffolding, and questions about scaffolding that are ripe for further investigation by researchers and practitioners.

Lepper, Drake, and O'Donnell-Johnson provide detailed analyses of highly skilled tutors working one-to-one with students in Chapter 4, entitled "Scaffolding Techniques of Expert Human Tutors." All of the tutoring sessions focused on primary and upper elementary grade mathematics and were led by experienced adult tutors. The authors describe the general structure of the tutoring sessions, and analyze how the tutors reacted to student errors. A central message of the chapter is that good tutors set out to boost students' confidence, sense of ability to meet challenges, curiosity, control, and self-efficacy as well as to help them learn. The characteristics of successful tutors are summarized with the acronym INSPIRE, which stands for Intelligent, Nurturant, Socratic, Progressively demanding, Indirect, Reflective, and Encouraging. The elements of scaffolding presented in this chapter are particularly useful with students who have difficulty and low self-efficacy in the subject area, but also could be useful ways to approach scaffolding with any group of students.

In contrast to Lepper and colleagues' focus on expert tutors, Graesser, Bowers, Hacker, and Person look at the dialogue patterns and pedagogical strategies of unskilled tutors in Chapter 5, "An Anatomy of Naturalistic Tutoring." They summarize analyses of a large corpus of sessions of graduate students tutoring undergraduates, and high school students tutoring seventh-graders on topics that are difficult for the students to understand. Their analyses reveal that unskilled tutors can be effective. This calls into question whether practices that have been assumed to be necessary for promoting student learning, such as sophisticated pedagogical strategies and accurate diagnosis of students' knowledge states, are in fact necessary. Instead, more basic strategies such as extensive use of examples and explanatory reasoning to elaborate and organize the material may be sufficient. Although the chapter raises the interesting possibility that effective scaffolding may not be as difficult as we think, the authors also acknowledge that their findings do not indicate that tutoring effects would not improve if tutors did use more sophisticated techniques. The news that unskilled tutors can effectively guide students' learning should be encouraging not only for teachers who are just learning how to scaffold, but also with regard to the use of peer tutors and computer tutors, neither of which can perform sophisticated diagnoses of a student's learning problems.

The illustrations of scaffolding in these chapters should fuel researchers' and practitioners' enthusiasm for discovering more about scaffolding. Scaffolding is an extremely social form of instruction, with peers and teachers interacting closely with a student as she or he attempts a task. To be successful, scaffolding requires a convivial atmosphere in which students can let their defenses down, and in which teachers make students feel at ease to take intellectual risks. When these conditions are met, scaffolding helps to create thoughtful environments where both teachers and students are thinking deeply about classroom tasks.

Our brief descriptions of the chapters in this book do not do justice to the insights contained in them. We invite you to read further, and hope that you will find the material as thought-provoking as we have.

CHAPTER ONE

Scaffolding: A Powerful Tool in Social Constructivist Classrooms

LAURA R. ROEHLER, Michigan State University

DANISE J. CANTLON, Holt Public Schools

After her students had had a year of opportunities to scaffold one another's learning, a teacher asked the whole class why they liked helping each other.

> KURT: I like to work with other people because it helps me learn to cooperate.
>
> KALLI: We get to share ideas together. We learn new things from others and we can give ideas too.
>
> MAURIE: I agree. It's fun helping out other kids. People help me because I help them.
>
> LINDA: When I work with others, they help me understand.

This group of elementary school students valued the opportunity that scaffolding provided for their learning. Why is scaffolding a valuable tool for teaching and learning? What is the role of scaffolding during learning conversations? How do children learn to have authentic learning conversations with one another? What are the important components of a social constructivist classroom?

To answer these questions, this chapter provides background information on the connectedness of social constructivism, scaffolding, and learning conversations within the context of the literacy cycle. Following this, the methods and results of our study are presented. The two guiding questions we use to examine the role of scaffolding are:

a. What *types* of scaffolding occurred during learning conversations?
b. What were the *characteristics* of scaffolding within a classroom setting?

The conclusions will summarize and expand the findings regarding these two questions.

BACKGROUND

Teachers and educators are realizing that future adults need to be self-reliant, adaptive, lifelong learners who can reason through problem-framing and problem-solving situations collaboratively. These adults need to be able to think and act in ways which signal that they value themselves and others, know how to be responsible for themselves and others, and are respectful of themselves and others.

Productive, effective youth of today and adults of tomorrow are different from the productive, effective youth and adults of yesterday. Until recently, educating young people primarily involved the *transmission* of knowledge. We believed there was a fixed knowledge base, and a teacher's responsibility was to give that knowledge to those who were learning. This called for the development of well-organized, clearly composed information that comprised this knowledge base. Literacy was conceptualized as a stable collection of hierarchical skills to be mastered. Drawing on the educational paradigm reflected in the views of behaviorism and information processing, the teacher's drill provided practice of isolated skills that led to mastery. The students' goal was to decode text and get meaning. The teacher's job was to provide students with rules and skills to obtain that goal. Lecture and recitation were the most common formats of instruction.

However, this way of thinking about teaching and learning has changed to a conception that students actively construct their own knowledge and understandings. They do this by making connections, building mental schemata, and developing new concepts from previous understandings. Instead of learning a set knowledge base, students develop evolving knowledge bases through interactions with others, requiring an active involvement in learning.

Helping students develop evolving knowledge bases through interactions is best achieved by using the *social constructivist* model (Gavelek, 1986; Smagorinski, 1995; Vygotsky, 1978; Wertsch, Mc-Namee, McLare, & Budwig, 1980). The social constructivist model assumes all knowledge is social in nature. Learning occurs in a context of social interactions leading to understanding. Learners are active risk takers who accept challenges and understand how and why to learn. They are given opportunities to restructure information in ways that make sense to them. Learners connect new material with their previously known information. They generate questions and comments as information becomes internalized. Learners first experience active problem-solving activities with others, but gradually become independent problem solvers. Initially, the teacher or more knowledgeable person controls and guides the learners' activities. Eventually, the teacher and learners share the responsibilities, with the learners taking the lead. The teacher continues to guide the learners' emerging understandings, providing assistance as needed. Finally, the teacher gives the full range of responsibilities to the learners by removing all assistance. This progression from someone else being responsible for the learning to the students being responsible for themselves is an appropriate way to create an effective sequence of learning. This internalization process begins on a social plane and moves to an inner plane where information becomes part of each individual's evolving knowledge base.

Within the social constructivist perspective, the area in which an individual's optimum learning can occur is called the *zone of proximal development* (ZPD). The ZPD is defined by Wertsch (1985) as:

the distance between the child's actual developmental level as determined by independent problem solving and the higher level of
potential development as determined through problem solving under adult guidance and in collaboration with more capable peers.

(pp. 67-68)

Thus, learning is the development of higher-level psychological
processes occurring first on an interpersonal level through social
interaction and later internalized. Within any given classroom, the
ZPD is determined by the learners' levels of development and the
forms of instruction. In all cases, instruction must proceed develop-
mentally, so that the learners are completing tasks they would be
unable to do without assistance. Each person's range of potential for
learning is shaped by the social environment in which it takes place.

Assistance in the zone of proximal development is called *scaffolding* and is a major component of teaching activity (see Bruner, 1984).
Scaffolding characterizes the social interaction among students and
teachers that precedes internalization of the knowledge, skills and
dispositions deemed valuable and useful for the learners. It is an
instructional tool that reduces learning ambiguity, thereby increasing
growth opportunities (Doyle, 1986). Scaffolding is described by
Wood, Bruner, and Ross (1976) as "... controlling those elements of
the task that are initially beyond the learner's capability, thus permitting him to concentrate upon and complete only those elements that
are within his range of competence" (p. 9). As the teacher or more
knowledgeable person creates a supporting structure that can initiate
and sustain interest, the students become involved. As the students
gradually gain control of the task, they take over more of the
responsibility. When the assumption of responsibility and control
occurs, the teacher removes the scaffolding.

Successful scaffolded instruction requires establishing *intersubjectivity* (Rommetveit, 1974), or a shared understanding of the task.
Teachers are responsible for leading the learners toward this understanding and helping them develop their own conception of the task.
This is done by creating a balance of support and challenge. Support

is provided through scaffolding; challenge is provided through learner interest in completing the task. Learners are given opportunities to *act like* they know how to complete a task before they actually do. Scaffolding and challenge need to be presented holistically and in a context that signals value and usefulness. This allows the integrity of the task to be maintained throughout the teaching and learning opportunities. Teachers and learners co-construct understandings about the task, enabling shared understanding to develop.

Scaffolding—developed to help students internalize information—best occurs in learning situations where the learners have opportunities to communicate their thoughts. Conversations provide such opportunities. Jane Roland Martin (1985) states,

> A good conversation is neither a fight nor a contest. Circular in form, cooperative in manner and constructive in intent, it is an interchange of ideas by those who see themselves not as adversaries but as human beings come together to talk and listen and learn from one another.
>
> (p. 10)

Conversation is a dialogic process by which we create and negotiate knowledge with one another. It is the primary means for solving higher-order problems and developing thinking strategies in those with less expertise, especially within the areas of reading (Duffy, Roehler, & Rackliffe, 1986; Pearson, 1985); writing (DiPardo & Freedman, 1988); mathematics (Lampert, 1990); and science (Palincsar, Anderson, & David, 1993).

A particular type of conversation called *instructional conversation* has been researched by Gallimore and Tharp (1990) in collaboration with Goldenberg (1991). They define instructional conversations as discussion-based lessons geared toward creating opportunities for students' conceptual and linguistic development. The teachers focus on concepts that are relevant for students and of some educational value. Background information on a topic is activated; teachers build on the students' ideas, and then guide the students to new levels of understanding. The teacher's responsibility is the facilitation of oral and written discourse in meaningful and/or useful ways. Instructional converstions act as metascripts (Gallimore & Tharp, 1990) in that a format is used that provides a structure for the discussions. This structure enhances learning.

Roehler and her associates have further refined the concept of conversations from instructional conversations to *learning conversations* (Roehler, Hallenback, McLellan, & Svoboda, 1996). Learning conversations are similar to instructional conversations but go one step further. In both types of conversations, teachers focus on concepts that are relevant for students and have educational value. Background information on a topic is activated while teachers build on the students' ideas and guide the students to new levels of understanding. However, in learning conversations, teachers do not merely teach; they also learn. They co-construct information with the students and gain new knowledge. They join conversations in which all ideas, comments, and questions are important. All participants value and respect their own ideas and the ideas of others. They also feel responsible for their own learning and the learning of others (Roehler, McLellan, & Svoboda, 1993). Learning for both students and teachers is the primary outcome.

Learning conversations became the means for explaining scaffolding in two classrooms where the social constructivist approach was implemented and maintained. The zones of proximal development for the two sets of students were used to consciously shape the learning opportunities through scaffolding as thematic units of instruction unfolded.

This study explored the role of scaffolding in two social constructivist classrooms. The first question we considered examined the *types* of scaffolding that occurred in learning conversations within language units. The second question explored the *characteristics* of scaffolding within a contextualized setting.

METHODS

Participants

The participants are teachers and students from two classrooms in two school districts during a three-year study.* Both classrooms were selected because they evidenced a social constructivist approach to teaching and learning. Scaffolding for the study occurred during language instruction. The first classroom was located in a suburban school district just outside a Midwestern city. It was a multi-age classroom comprised of fifty third-, fourth-, and fifth-graders and two teachers. The student population was diverse, especially with regard to the socioeconomic range, with 23% of the students receiving free or reduced lunch. Ethnically, only 5% of the student body was classified as minorities. About 70% of the students had been in the multi-age room for at least two years. One classroom teacher had been teaching for nineteen years, and the second classroom teacher had been teaching for six years. Both taught mathematics and social studies. One teacher instructed all language literacy lessons; the other taught all the science lessons.

The second classroom in the study was also located in a suburban school district just outside a Midwestern city. It was an English as Second Language (ESL) classroom composed of students from Korea, the People's Republic of China/Taiwan, Estonia, India, Malaysia, the Czech Republic, and Russia. They were all first-year English language learners ranging from the third through the fifth grade. The upper-level classes were selected because the students' oral English expertise was proficient enough for conversations to occur. Most of the students received reduced or free lunches. The teachers included two ESL teachers—one of whom had been teaching for 22 years, the other for 21 years—and one university professor, who had been involved in classroom instruction for 26 years. The ESL teachers were

---

* The teachers involved in this study were Danise Cantlon and Pamela Seales in the multi-age classroom, and Meredith McLellan, Laura Roehler, and Nancy Svoboda in the ESL classroom.

responsible for the instruction of ESL students one hour at a time, five times a week. The university professor joined the ESL teachers for one class period three or four times a week.

Setting

The multi-age classroom was located in a K–5 school, in two classrooms that were connected through an opening in the wall. The learning environment of this classroom was collaborative in nature, providing continuous opportunities for social interaction among all learners. Throughout the day, students and teachers had time to create questions and research topics, create and solve problems, learn content, and share ideas as they constructed meaning. Verbal interactions among students created opportunities for them to have a vested interest in one another's learning. The students saw their ideas, explanations, and teaching as valuable and useful to the learning of their classmates. Mutual respect and responsibility were essential to the learning community. Scaffolding was provided and reduced as students internalized dispositions about themselves as learners, the reasoning process, and the new content knowledge.

The ESL classroom was located in a K–5 public school set within a married housing unit of a major university. The students were children of undergraduate and graduate students attending the university. Many had known little or no English when they first arrived from over forty different countries. While a few were from single-parent families, many were children of first-generation college students. A number of international students' families were sponsored by their home governments. The learning environment of the ESL classroom was based on learning conversations that provided continuous interactions among teachers and learners. Throughout the hour-long class period, students and teachers had time to frame and solve problems, generate questions and comments about the contents of the lessons, gain understandings, and share ideas. The teachers created opportunities for students to value and respect one another's learning by providing for co-constructed verbal interactions. Students saw their ideas, thoughts, and feelings as valuable to all participants. Scaffolding was provided and reduced as students gained control and became responsible for learning valuable and useful knowledge, skills, and dispositions.

A Description of the Teaching and Learning Experience

The teaching and learning experiences in both classrooms were designed to focus on learning conversations within the literacy cycle (Duffy & Roehler, 1993). The literacy cycle provided many opportunities to talk, read, and write in structured settings. Conversations played a major role within this cycle as students' expertise in reading and writing grew. Since it is known that knowledge is generally acquired in social situations, and since students already talked to family members, friends, and acquaintances on an ongoing, comfortable basis, the structure of learning conversations was used.

The literacy cycle was initiated with guided reading and writing. During this time, teachers created opportunities to read, write, and then talk about student- and teacher-selected topics, using a Book Club format (Raphael, Goatley, McMahon, & Woodman, 1995). Reading and writing activities included such formats as books, journals, poems, magazines, and newspaper articles. Videos and CD-ROMs were watched and discussed. Learning conversations were combined with these literacy events, ultimately leading to the creation of rough drafts—including stories, articles, poems, and books—written both individually and in groups. Specific, explicit, and adaptive instruction in reading and writing occurred as needed within learning conversations.

If students wanted to share their beginning ideas and seek additional ideas, or had difficulty in creating rough drafts, they joined a group at a *Sharing Area* where students and/or teachers met to discuss the emerging rough drafts. Reading and writing activities and learning conversations occurred at this time. Students returned to the sharing area to revise as needed. Eventually, students took their latest drafts to an *Editing Area* where the collaborative teaching team and/

or the students provided assessment of content, mechanics, and form. Once again, reading, writing, and conversations occurred. After teachers and students assessed the written products, the students shared the final drafts at the *Author's Chair* within learning conversations, and the literacy cycle began again. Ongoing, authentic reading, writing, and learning conversations occurred continuously throughout this literacy cycle.

In both classrooms, teachers collaboratively created and implemented literacy lessons within integrated thematic units, using the structure of the literacy cycle. The students were expected to be constructively responsive participants who could co-construct knowledge within oral and written discourse. The classrooms involved much sharing, interaction, valuing, respecting of self and others, and development of responsibility for self and others. All participants had equal status, with varying degrees of expertise about school-related issues.

Data Collection and Analysis

Over three years in the two classrooms, the authors collected data in the forms of student interviews, teacher journal excerpts, audiotaped lessons, field notes of literacy lessons, and transcripts of literacy lessons. They also completed student interviews for each marking period and kept daily teacher journals. Literacy lessons were taped within month-long units and subsequently transcribed. Field notes were mostly taken on a daily basis.

In addressing the two research questions, qualitative methods were used. The *constant comparative* method (Glaser, 1978; Glaser & Strauss, 1967) was selected. One university professor, two graduate students, and two teachers analyzed the data. The major analysis consisted of a three-stage process relying primarily on the transcribed lessons. The field notes, teacher journals, and student journals provided ways to cross-check and revise hypotheses arising from lesson transcripts. This process of triangulation (Gorden, 1980) strengthened the hypotheses.

During the *first stage*, lesson transcripts were read and reread to capture the events and the flow of conversations. The beginnings and endings of learning conversations were noted and conversations were labeled. Field notes were used to verify the learning conversations. During the *second stage*, the contents of learning conversations were analyzed to yield examples of scaffolding and a description of contextualized scaffolding. This analysis identified categories of scaffolding that were being used and offered possible descriptions of contextualized scaffolding. These contextualized characteristics and types of scaffolding were shared with other coders to seek agreement and create definitions. The process of coding, seeking, and creating characteristics and examples then continued. During the *third stage*, the examples of scaffolding were grouped and the contextualized descriptions were noted. As new descriptions of the contextualized scaffolding were modified and new types of scaffolding were found, the previously coded contextualized characteristics and examples of scaffolding were recoded.

RESULTS

The results of the analysis are reported in terms of the two research questions. In both classrooms, scaffolding was embedded in learning conversations that reflected the social constructivist model.

Types of Scaffolding

The first research question examined the *types* of scaffolding that occurred within the two classrooms. Lesson transcripts from the ESL classroom were used to answer this question.

The analysis yielded five different types of scaffolding designed to help students gain conceptual understandings. These five types occurred as students were learning in their zones of proximal development. This learning began with information sharing, in which the raw material for constructing understanding was communicated, and then moved to mediated learning, in which the learners gradually took responsibility and control of their learning (Roehler & Duffy, 1991).

Offering explanations. The first type of scaffolding consisted of *explanations.* Explanations are explicit statements adjusted to fit the learners' emerging understandings about what is being learned (*declarative* or *prepositional knowledge*), why and when it is used (*conditional* or *situational knowledge*), and how it is used (*procedural knowledge*) (Duffy, Roehler, Meloth, & Vavrus, 1986; Paris, Lipson, & Wixson, 1983).

An example of explanations occurred in the ESL classroom in a unit on animals and their behavior. Teacher A began a class period with an explanation of the responsibilities of the author and the listeners during Author's Chair, when students read their writings to others. These responsibilities had been discussed before, but the teachers had assessed that learning had not yet occurred. Teacher A prompted the students to recall what they were to learn about being listeners. She then asked them to remember how a listener acts. The students replied that listeners should look at the people who are talking, be polite, and not talk or raise their hands when others are talking. The teacher and the students provided information about what listeners were and how they behaved. The generated responsibilities were listed by Teacher B. Teacher A continued by providing an explanation of why it was important for listeners to help authors feel comfortable when reading in the Author's Chair.

TEACHER A: All of those things make the person giving the report feel more comfortable, doesn't it? Because if you're giving your report and people are showing you in ways that they can that they're interested and that they like your report, then that makes you more comfortable, doesn't it? And you can say, "Oh, this is fun. I like sharing this because other people are signaling to me they'd like to hear it."

Throughout the remainder of the lesson, the teachers gradually removed the explanations about what listeners do, how they do it, and why that behavior is important.

Inviting student participation. The second type of scaffolding was inviting student participation. In this type of scaffolding, learners were given opportunities to join in the process that was occurring. After the teacher provided illustrations of some of the thinking, feelings, or actions that were needed to complete the task, the learners had opportunities to fill in the pieces they knew and understood. This type of scaffolding occurred in the following lesson excerpt.

Teacher A continued the lesson by helping the students learn how to be good authors. She invited them to participate by suggesting behaviors that were appropriate for the author during Author's Chair.

TEACHER A: Maybe we should now have us think about how to behave as the author during Author's Chair. What do authors do? Who can remember? Would you like to start?

TINA: The author sits in the Author's Chair and speaks loud and clear.

CRYSTAL: The author should not fool around like making faces or having outside conversations.

SHINA: The author should not be shy and should be brave and confident.

Teachers continued to invite students to participate in the subsequent lessons as this type of scaffolding, *inviting participation*, was gradually removed. A list of responsibilities was created and used in subsequent lessons.

Verifying and clarifying student understandings. In the third type of scaffolding, teachers checked the students' emerging understandings. If the emerging understandings were reasonable, the teacher verified the students' responses. If the emerging understandings were not reasonable, the teacher offered clarification. This type of scaffolding, *verifying and clarifying student understandings,* was also found in excerpts from the animal behavior unit. Conversations continued to focus on Author's Chair.

Teacher A acknowledged the students' good efforts and asked all participants if the list of author's responsibilities made sense. When she had verified that they understood, she asked the students to generate listeners' responsibilities in the same way. After the list had been generated, she asked the students to make decisions about another responsibilities list created earlier in the year. They were to note any listener responsibilities on the earlier list that had not been listed this time.

TEACHER A: Now, are there any in the earlier list that we don't have on our current list? Yes, Shina.

SHINA: The audience may try to show that they enjoyed what the authors said.

TEACHER A: We hadn't talked about that. That's important, isn't it? To show that we enjoyed it. What else was new? Crystal.

CRYSTAL: I think that the audience should be ready ... ready to ask questions or offer or have comments when the author stops sharing.

TEACHER B: That was one that we just barely thought about, but that's really important, isn't it? It may be one of the most important things about the audience's responsibility that you need to think about. Like, "Oh, I like this part because it reminds me of such and such," or "I wonder what this means?" Or, "I wonder what would happen if all those types of things would happen." It is really fun to share those types of questions and comments. Now does this make sense? Okay, Tina, did you have your hand up earlier?

TINA: The audience should be thinking of a comment or question for the author?

TEACHER A: That's a good one too. Sometimes that is hard to do, isn't it? To think and listen at the same time. Okay?

TINA: How do you do that?

TEACHER A: Sometimes people have a piece of paper to jot it down. That's okay too. If you feel like you want to have a piece of paper, then we can do that. Any others? So, do you think we are ready for Author's Chair?

In this lesson transcript, students shared their understandings and the teachers verified those understandings. Effort was acknowledged, and the knowledge was signaled as important and useful. When confusion was indicated, the teacher provided information.

Modeling of desired behaviors. The fourth type of scaffolding was *modeling*—defined as a teaching behavior that showed how one should feel, think, or act within a given situation (Duffy, Roehler, & Herrmann, 1988). It included *think-aloud* modeling, or demonstrating to learners the thought processes underlying successive steps in a task. One example of think-aloud modeling was a school activity in which participants were deciding what was important in a book chapter, and a teacher thought aloud about the reasoning that is used. Modeling also included *talk-alouds*, in which the designated teacher showed the learners how to act by talking through the steps of the task as it was completed. In one example of talk-aloud modeling, a teacher talked about the picture clues in a particular story, but not about the reasoning needed to understand the story. Finally, in *performance modeling,* the learners were simply shown how to carry out a task, with no think-alouds or talk-alouds about the performance or the progress toward completing the performance. The school activity in which the teacher reads silently as the students read silently (known as USSR/Uninterrupted Sustained Silent Reading or DEAR/Drop Everything and Read) was an example of performance modeling. In this type of modeling, the teacher physically demonstrated reading and the enjoyment of the reading material by laughing, smiling, etc. (See Roehler & Duffy, 1991, for a more detailed explanation of the types of modeling.)

The modeling in our analysis broke down into two main functions. The first was *making thinking visible*, as with think-aloud modeling. In this process, participants think through their emerging understanding of a process out loud as they make attempts to solve a problem or issue. In this form of scaffolding, teachers modeled think-alouds of their approach to a task, and learners were encouraged to do the same. This process is difficult and usually occurs after a number of students have contributed clues.

In the following lesson excerpt, the group was talking about creating weather myths. A teacher thought aloud about the mythical reasons for volcanoes and prepared the students for the next learning event.

TEACHER B: That's the end of that one. You know what I was wondering? What caused that volcano to bubble like that? Can you think of a reason why? It would have to be something inside of the volcano, wouldn't it? What caused the lava to get hot and bubble over like that? What is the reason for the inside of the volcano to be hot? To be heated up. Let's think, if we could imagine anything that we wanted. Could we say that the volcano was a cooking pot for somebody and there was a big fire underneath there? What do you think? Any other ideas? What would be causing that volcano? Maybe, we could be thinking about that when we watch the next piece of videotape?

Later in the lesson, a student made her thinking visible when thinking aloud about how night occurs.

SARI: I have one for night.
TEACHER B: Okay.
SARI: The ... um ... a giant girl, she has ... she has ... She likes black so she wears it and she has long, long black hair.
TINA: A black lady?
SARI: No, a girl, she like black.
TEACHER A: A girl, she likes black. A girl that likes black.
SARI: Have long hair.
TEACHER A: Has long black hair, right?
SARI: Yeah. And when she runs, her hair goes like that, and then ... it flows. And it's night.

In this last excerpt, Sari was able to think aloud her reason for the occurrence of night: a girl with long dark flowing hair causes it.

The second type of modeling found in the analysis was the *modeling of question and comment generation*. This falls into the category of talk-aloud modeling. The following example lesson was a continuation of the unit on animal behavior using the Author's Chair format. Different students read reports, one at a time, while all the others listened. All participants tried to enact the responsibilities of authors and listeners. Listeners were specifically encouraged to generate comments and ask questions during each reading. The first sharing was a report on elephants. After the report was shared, the teachers modeled the talk-aloud strategy of generating questions and making comments. In the following excerpt, Teacher B modeled a comment.

TEACHER B: I think it was interesting when you talked about the baby elephant—that they were three feet high when they were born. And, they weighed ...

TINA: Two hundred.

TEACHER B: Two to three hundred pounds. These are very big babies. And, also, I was interested in the hair. When babies are born, they have hair covering their bodies. I didn't realize that. I was also amazed they can walk in an hour.

Teacher B supported the student's efforts and was specific in her comments about the report.

Teachers also modeled questions about the elephants. Teacher A asked a question about types of elephants.

TEACHER A: I was wondering if you ... know which kinds of elephants those are in the picture. Are those Indian elephants or African ones?

After this question had been discussed, Teacher B followed the conversation with the modeling of another question.

TEACHER B: I was wondering what a land animal is? In your report, you had that an elephant is a land animal.

This led to an extended conversation about land animals and examples of land animals. During this conversation, a student said that elephants can pick up everything with their trunks. Teacher A then modeled an elaborated comment about the muscles in elephants' trunks.

TEACHER A: That's what I was thinking of with all those muscles. Their trunks can go up over their heads. They can also go straight out and then they can curl all the way down and back. So, they really have tremendous flexibility.

TINA: Shina.

SHINA: We have the hand. Maybe they use the trunk for carrying something, like our hands.

TEACHER B: That's right. Like we use the hands, they use their trunks.

The student emulated the teacher's elaborated comment and connected the information to knowledge she already had.

After extended conversations based on participants' comments and questions about Tina's report on elephants, Teacher B modeled supportive feedback about the process of generating questions and comments during Author's Chair.

TEACHER B: It amazes me when we have our reports and we share them. I feel we could start writing all over again on the same subject. Because, as we're discussing the elephant and the more we talk about it together, the more questions and comments that come to mind. This happens regularly. We really get to talk and learn all about our reports.

A second report on elephants was read in Author's Chair. The author then opened the conversation for questions and comments. The students began the comments and questions so teacher modeling was not needed.

CRYSTAL: Yes.

SELON: Your report was good and what ... what was the question in the

> beginning?

CRYSTAL: In the beginning, how do elephants feel when people ride or sit on them?

SELON: Not this one, the first one.

CRYSTAL: Okay. How do elephants' mothers take care of them ... or the little babies?

At this time, the students' comments were not elaborated and the questions were not opportunities to connect content information, so Teacher A modeled a connecting content question with an elaborated comment.

TEACHER B: I was wondering when you said that the mother elephant has the baby elephant inside her for twenty or twenty-two months. Does it stay in there that long because it has to have more time? It's so big when it is born.

CRYSTAL: I don't know. But I think that ... yes, it might be that because ...

TEACHER B: That's a long time.

CRYSTAL: Yes.

TINA: Human beings have just nine months.

SELON: Yeah, so I think it's longer.

TEACHER B: You said twenty or twenty-two ... that would be more than a year.

TINA: Double!

TEACHER B: Just a little less than two years. Wow!

CRYSTAL: Almost two years that she carry her baby. Yes.

TINA: I think the baby elephant has ... have to stay in her mother's body for that long, because it has to grow ... grow long.

CRYSTAL: Maybe.

SELON: In Tina's report she said that ... uh ... it can walk after an hour. Maybe it's that way because it stays so long in the mother's ... body.

TEACHER A: Good thinking!

TEACHER B: I hadn't thought of putting those two things together.

A teacher opened this learning conversation with a modeling of a question and a comment that connected content. Tina and Selon offered elaborated comments that signaled they had made connections in their knowledge, with Selon showing that she had made connections from two different sources. The teachers continued to model elaborated comments and questions that helped the students to offer their own comments and questions. Scaffolding decreased as learning occurred.

A third report was then read in Author's Chair. Shina read her report on pandas. Student questions and comments followed.

> SHINA: The panda is kind of big animal. The name panda came from the mountain country of Nepal. Panda look like bears and pandas are black and white. Pandas have colorful teeth. When we touch them they are soft. Pandas are not dangerous animals. Panda have poor eyesight. Black and white pandas really have sharp teeth, too. Pandas have the larger teeth than other ... any other animal. The first panda lived about a million years ago. Panda live in China always. Panda's moms take care of the baby by holding the baby ... by holding the panda or baby in the mother's arms and holding the baby all the time whenever she goes. Pandas sleep 12 to 15 hours a day. Pandas eat grasses and roots and leaves. But their favorite food is leaves. This report talks about the descriptions and behaviors of pandas. I write about how they live, where they live, what they eat, what they like and how they take care of their babies.

Student-generated questions and comments followed.

> SELON: What did you say their favorite food was?
> SHINA: Leaves. [pause] Crystal?
> CRYSTAL: Okay. I have three questions. What country to they ... was living?
> SHINA: Nepal.
> CRYSTAL: They living ... always in what country?

SHINA: China.

CRYSTAL: China? Okay.

TINA: No, where did they come from?

SHINA: Oh, the name? The name of the place? They come from the mountainous country of Nepal.

TINA: Where is it?

TEACHER A: That's a good question.

SELON: Probably China.

CRYSTAL: And, where panda live?

SHINA: China.

CRYSTAL: China. Okay. And does the baby eat ... where ... he first, he looks or he eats already leaves? I mean, some type of animals, they ... first eat mother's milk, and then eat leaves.

SHINA: First, they eat ... um ... the mother's milk and they eat, they grow and they eat leaves.

SELON: I like the way ... how you described that. You put it in order.

SHINA: Uh, Crystal?

CRYSTAL: I really like your report and you covered a lot of information about panda.

SHINA: Thank you.

The students were responsible for this entire conversation using elaborated comments and questions that provided opportunities for ongoing knowledge connections. Teacher A verified the value of a question only once. The students continued to be responsible for the content of the learning conversations as Shina made a comment about her report.

SHINA: When I go to library ... um ... I took a panda book. I read yesterday and they tell when the panda eats. And, they say the panda always eat in the night.

CRYSTAL: Yeah, they do. They do eat at night.

TINA: Why is that?

SHINA: Maybe that's ... that's the time when every ... animal go in their houses.

SELON: I think I know.

CRYSTAL: Maybe they eat like, maybe before they can sleep ... with something inside.

SHINA: I don't know. Maybe they have no breakfast, lunch, and dinner.

SELON: I think I know why they eat at night. Because then nobody could see them resting and eating and everything. So, like people can't kill them more at night so they just go out and eat at night.

SHINA: Crystal.

CRYSTAL: I think they're hiding because maybe people, so many people, they kill them. And so, they hiding in the day somewhere so all day he ... she have to carry her baby. Then, at night, when everybody sleeps, they know that peoples are sleeping. They can go and eat outside and do anything that they want. Have change from days.

SHINA: I have a question about eyesight. I'm not really sure what that means.

During earlier lesson segments, the teachers modeled connective questions and elaborated comments. The students gradually took control and eventually, the learning conversations were led by the students' comments and questions.

Inviting students to contribute clues. The fifth type of scaffolding was one in which several students contributed clues for reasoning through the issue or problem. In this form of scaffolding, learners were encouraged to offer clues about how to complete the task. Together, the teachers and students verbalized the process.

An earlier conversation about mythical reasons for weather events continued with the teachers showing how to contribute ideas. One teacher invited participation, and a second teacher contributed a clue. The first teacher then connected the clue.

TEACHER B: Is air a natural event?

TEACHER C: Good question. It just happens out there, doesn't it? Have any thoughts on why it would have to come out? Be creative, have fun.

TEACHER B: Stretch.

TEACHER C: Okay. So the inside of the earth is stretching. So, it stretches so far that it pushes out. The earth is stretching. I like that. Any other ideas about why that stuff bubbles out of the mountain?

This lesson continued as students and teachers brainstormed weather events. In the next day's lesson, students began to take responsibility for contributing the clues.

In this segment, the participants continued a learning conversation about the mythical reasons for the weather events of a blizzard.

TINA: What's causing a blizzard?

SARI: You know ... um ... the king of North Pole, the king of North Pole came here and got mad because ... um ...

TEACHER A: Came here where it's warm.

TEACHER C: Came here where it's warm, got mad. So?

TINA: 'Cause he likes cold.

TEACHER C: So he ...

TEACHER A: And so, what did he do to make the blizzard?

SELON: He cried.

SHINA: ... his tears turn into snow and the wind ...

TEACHER A: He cried very hard, right? And, his tears turned into?

SHINA: Snow.

TEACHER C: Snow. And, his ... ?

SELON: Maybe his tears turn into sleet?

TEACHER C: Uh huh. There you go!

TEACHER C: Okay. I have the king of the North Pole came here where it's warm and he?

SARI: Was mad.

TEACHER C: Was mad. And cried hard.

TEACHER A: Yes, very hard.

SELON: Cried very hard.

SARI: And ... um ... his tears turned to sleet and snow and ... um ... his ...

TEACHER C: His breath turned into wind?

STUDENTS: Yeah.

Later in the lesson, the students took most of the responsibility for contributing clues. They were talking about reasons for snow.

SARI: Just tell a little bit of your idea.

SHINA: Um ... snowflakes ... um ... stars are making good.

TEACHER B: Why are they falling to the ground?

SHINA: Maybe, because they drop.

TEACHER B: They dropped what? They dropped their cookies? Okay.

CRYSTAL: How come snowflakes is always the same? Like they all have six sides.

SHINA: I don't know.

TEACHER A: Can you imagine?

SHINA: 'Cause ... um ... the stars ... maybe, the stars want to pattern six point things but they only have five. So ... cookies with six sides are dropped.

TEACHER A: Cookies with six sides. That's very good. You are being creative.

SARI: Maybe the stars want to have five ... six point like that but they only have five so they make their cookies six.

Later still in the lesson, the students took full responsibility for contributing clues.

TINA: I got one. The eclipse is the sun and moon kissing.

SELON: What?

TINA: The sun and the moon is kissing.
[laughter]

SELON: Don't write that down.

CRYSTAL: It should be bumping into each other.

TEACHER C: Oh, I have to finish writing *[on large paper]*. You want me to write kissing?

SELON: Just write the k-word.

TEACHER C: Well, we can change it?

STUDENTS: Yeah.

STUDENTS: No.

    SELON: Wait, I know one. I know what it should be … it could be bumping into each other.

    CRYSTAL: Yeah, I think that's right.

    TINA: Oh yeah, bumping.

TEACHER C: Do you want to change it to bumping?

STUDENTS: Yeah.

In summary, five types of scaffolding occurred. The teachers *offered explanations, invited student participation, verified and clarified student understandings, modeled* making thinking visible and the generation of questions and comments, and *invited students to contribute clues.* These types of scaffolding were reduced as the students gained responsibility for their learning. Eventually, the students were in control, signaling that they had internalized ways to contribute to the conversations.

Description of a Scaffolded Learning Opportunity

Our second research question looked at a learning opportunity where contextualized scaffolding occurred. As types of scaffolding occurred within contextualized events, they were noted. In the multi-age classroom, a unit on tall tales was implemented. The comparison thinking strategy was introduced at the beginning of the unit. On the first day, "Annie Christmas," taken from *Cut from the Same Cloth* (San Souci & Pinckney, 1993), was read to the whole group. A conversation about the literary elements, the tall tale genre (including exaggerations), and affective responses occurred. The types of scaffolding included explanations and inviting student participation.

On the following day, "Bess Call," also taken from *Cut from the Same Cloth,* was read. Before the reading occurred, comparisons were discussed. One of the teachers explained the comparison strategy using an example of cats and dogs. The teacher used think-aloud modeling about how the two animals were alike and invited student participation as she made a list on the dryboard. Then she modeled as she thought out loud about how cats and dogs are different by reading a list. The students were helped to understand how comparisons are made by examining two familiar things to see how they are similar and/or different. After providing another example of making comparisons, the teacher again invited students to participate. At the end of the learning opportunity, the class generated a definition, "A comparison tells how things are the same or different." The students then contributed clues about comparisons.

> ALISSA: Comparisons are important because they make you think harder about the book.
>
> SEAN: You have to understand what is happening in both books to make a comparison so you learn more.
>
> CLAIRE: You use them by finding something in a book that is similar to another book. Or you can also tell how things are not the same. Or you can do both.
>
> KATHY: I think you should tell both how they are alike and different. That way you learn more about the two books.
>
> DEAN: First you read a tall tale, then you read another one. How you make your comparison is to think how they are the same or not. It's like making a connection between books you read. So anyways, it helps you understand more because you have to think about two things.

During this learning conversation, teachers provided explanations and modeling about why comparisons were used and how to make them. The goal was for all students to understand the meaning of a comparison, why it is an important strategy, and how to use it. The students were invited to join the process by creating a definition of a comparison. They then contributed clues as they applied this strategy while having conversations about the two tall tales.

After reading "Bess Call," the remaining whole-group time was spent with students giving examples of comparisons between Annie Christmas and Bess Call. In that conversation, Jack, Caitlin, and Peter used thinking aloud after the teachers had modeled it.

JACK: Both tall tales were about women who helped people take care of bullies.

CAITLIN: They were both about strong women who got what they wanted. The two tall tales were different because Annie whipped twelve men at once but Bess only wrestled one man.

PETER: Annie was a hero because she saved the people's lives on the boat during the storm. Bess wasn't a hero because she didn't save anybody's life.

After the whole-group conversations, the students moved into Book Clubs where they read, wrote, and talked about creating their own tall tales.

The next day, during whole-group conversations, a Venn diagram (Musser & Berger, 1988) was created using the two tall tales. The teacher first provided an explanation that a Venn diagram was a visual tool for making comparisons. Then, she modeled talk-alouds using a Venn diagram showing the cat and dog comparison (see Figure 1-1). The teacher talked about how the space under the cat

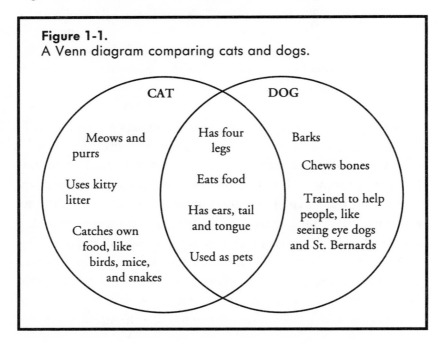

Figure 1-1.
A Venn diagram comparing cats and dogs.

CAT — DOG

Meows and purrs

Uses kitty litter

Catches own food, like birds, mice, and snakes

Has four legs

Eats food

Has ears, tail and tongue

Used as pets

Barks

Chews bones

Trained to help people, like seeing eye dogs and St. Bernards label was exclusively for cat characteristics, the space under the dog label was exclusively for dog characteristics, and the space where they overlapped was for characteristics common to both cats and dogs. She noted that the Venn diagram can be helpful because you can see at a glance how two things are alike (the overlap) or different (the separate space).

After the explanation and modeling, the tall tale "John Henry" (Keats, 1965) was compared to "Annie Christmas" using a Venn diagram. The students were invited to participate in a whole-group conversation about this activity as a Venn diagram was created. The following statements are students' contributions.

> ROBERT: John Henry was a railroad person but Annie wasn't. So put that idea under the separate part just about John Henry.
> SCOTT: You could put that Annie was a boatworker, alone in her spot.
> HANNAH: Annie was a black person, so write it in her circle.
> SARAH: I know something they both were. They both were black people. You can put that where the circles overlap in the middle. They both are black so it would go in the overlap, not just in Annie's section.

During this discussion, students made their thinking visible as they placed information in the Venn diagrams and explained their reasoning. The students also verified their understanding during the oral exchange. Sarah helped clarify why Hannah's idea belonged in the overlap space.

After whole-group conversations, the students picked a partner and created their own Venn diagram using two different tall tales they had read during Book Clubs. Their learning was scaffolded often by another student, and sometimes by a teacher. This scaffolding included contributing clues, making thinking visible, and verifying and clarifying each other's ideas with questions and comments as they brainstormed about the tall tale comparisons and explained the placement of the information on the Venn diagram.

Over the next month, written and oral responses during Book

Club focused on comparisons; students responded thoughtfully. Partners wrote comparisons between a tall tale and their own life. Conversations during Book Club provided opportunities for students to monitor their understandings about comparisons and to push other students to make more complete responses. One Book Club conversation illustrates how one student contributed clues to assist a peer.

RYAN: I am making a comparison to my own life and Pecos Bill. Pecos Bill is about a cowboy, who lives with the wolves. He rides a cyclone. He marries SlueFoot Sue.

DEMI: So what is the comparison? That sounds like a summary. You forgot to tell how you are like or different from Pecos Bill.

Demi monitored Ryan's understanding, challenged his thinking, and then contributed clues that enabled Ryan to better understand comparisons. His written response in his Book Club log reflected that he had enhanced his understandings about comparisons.

Another excerpt from a Book Club conversation follows. A teacher joined a group to model how to generate questions and make comments after she observed that the Book Club members were just reading their written responses with no listeners actively participating. She wanted them to have an authentic *conversation* instead of merely reporting from their written responses.

TEACHER: When I was listening to Maggie's responses, I was thinking about some questions and comments. I was wondering, why did Johnny Appleseed want to help people by planting apple seeds? I also had a comment for Maggie. I really like the way you made a connection between our tall tale unit and our historical fiction unit. You talked about our focus on the interaction between Native American Indians and settlers. Just like we learned that sometimes these two groups of people got along peacefully. Maggie is telling us about that idea in her tall tale book.

The students followed the teacher's modeling by generating their own questions and comments that verified and clarified each other's understanding.

> JEFF: Maggie, you did a nice job summarizing because you told some interesting details.
>
> MAGGIE: Thanks.
>
> MARIA: Was Johnny Appleseed the only tall tale about a real person? This tall tale didn't have as many exaggerations.
>
> MAGGIE: I'm not really sure. I think. . . John Henry was real.
>
> ZACK: I think a lot of tall tales were based on real people. But ... then, they added a lot of lies.
>
> MARIA: You mean exaggerations? Lies are different. They're mean. Exaggerations are for fun.

The Book Club group members gradually took responsibility for the learning conversations. They started asking questions and making comments to each other. They developed understandings by making their thinking visible, talking aloud, verifying and clarifying understandings, and contributing clues as their learning conversation evolved.

The final activity was for each student to write a comparison paper about Pecos Bill, based on the movie video and the written tall tale (Kellogg, 1986). A planning sheet for comparisons was explained and modeled. The teacher talked aloud about how to use a planning sheet, explaining that it was a way to organize thoughts on comparisons. The teacher used a planning sheet as she explained the procedure.

After watching the video, the students were invited to participate by contributing their clues about comparison in writing. For example, Denny's completed planning sheet showed reasonable comparisons between the movie and the book. For the first question, asking which two things were being compared, he wrote, "the movie of pacos [Pecos] bill [Bill]" and "the story of pacos [Pecos] bill [Bill]." For the second question, which asked how the two were alike, he wrote, "in both they lassod [lassoed] a tornado," "Slewfoot Sue rode a big catfish," and "the horse ate dynamite." For the third question, asking how they were different, he wrote, "In the book they were dying of bourdom [boredom]," "In the book bill [Bill] has a rope as long as the equater [equator]," "And in the movie he dident [didn't], thats [that's] different," and "bill [Bill] got kiked [kicked] out of texas [Texas]." Denny made his thinking visible when he completed his comparison paper. One teacher verified the accuracy of his contributions.

The following day, the students used their planning sheets to write rough drafts. Students met with their peer editors to ask questions and make comments about their partners' comparison papers. Teachers provided some scaffolding by modeling and explaining comparisons for students who were still attempting to make sense of comparisons. They again invited these students to participate by making their thinking visible in order to verify or clarify. They asked the students to contribute clues about comparisons. As the students carried on learning conversations, the teachers verified or clarified the students' emerging understandings. As the students' understandings of comparisons grew, the teachers' understandings of their students' understandings grew. The teachers reduced the scaffolding as students learned.

It should be noted that scaffolding was initiated and dropped at different times for different students. Learning did not occur uniformly with all the students. In the tall tale/comparison unit, the students showed that they were at varying points on the continuum toward internalizing the information as knowledge. After the comparison strategy was introduced, some students had grown to the point where they could apply the strategy as they read tall tales. Others could not and continued to need scaffolding. The teachers had to vary the scaffolding to best meet the needs of all students. Few of the students were at the same point at the same time in gaining responsibility and control of using the comparison strategy. The same variation occurred during the development of understandings about tall tales. Some students internalized the content knowledge about tall tales, while others still struggled; varying degrees of scaffolding remained for some students, while others operated on their own.

CONCLUSIONS

The students and teachers in these two classrooms created knowledge using strategic reasoning as desirable dispositions supported that learning. This learning occurred in opportunities that reflected the social constructivist model. As students explored questions and concerns of their own making, they felt responsible and in control of learning. Five types of scaffolding were found. Explanations and modeling were provided as needed. Students were invited to participate. As students made their thinking visible and generated questions and comments, their emerging understandings were verified and clarified. Gradual reduction of the scaffolding assisted students as they internalized the new content knowledge, the reasoning processes, and the dispositions of helping, valuing, and respecting self and others. The reduction of scaffolding occurred in a context which had to be taken into account when the data was analyzed.

The teachers in these two classrooms created contextualized learning opportunities that illustrated powerful learning principles. The first principle was the *balance of challenge and support*. The challenge was the learning of knowledge, strategies, and dispositions through activities that were of high interest for the students and included choice. These challenges created the intellectual unrest, or curiosity, needed for learning. Support was the assistance that the teachers provided during learning opportunities. This support was twofold: one type was permanent, the other temporary.

One type of permanent support was the use of the literacy cycle. It provided structured consistency, allowing the students to focus their cognitive energy on the learning of the new knowledge, skills, and dispositions embedded in the teaching-learning situations. Another type of permanent support was the use of the learning conversation format, which acted as a type of metascript (Gallimore & Tharpe, 1989). This support assisted teachers as they met the needs of their students.

Yet another type of permanent support was the teachers' modeling of *manner*. Manner consists of the dispositions and character traits of a person (Fenstermaker, 1992). Manner is shaped by habituation, learning opportunities, and reasoning about intentions and actions. Teachers developed manner in these students by showing them ways of thinking and acting, and providing them with opportunities to form habits of these approaches. Students responded in specific ways and were engaged in thinking about their actions and reflecting about them. The teachers in these two classrooms reflected the manner that Fenstermaker calls *effective and responsible teaching*. They promoted a respect for evidence, as well as a sense of tentativeness and willingness to suspend decisions while exploration proceeded. Their thinking and actions showed an appreciation of and regard for inquiry and an openness to alternative and competing ideas. They reflected a valuing of self and others, respect for self and others, and responsibility for self and others.

Temporary support, which was gradually removed, included the five types of scaffolding. Students learned when information was explained and modeled using think-alouds and talk-alouds. They also learned when they were invited to participate with the knowledge they possessed, no matter how rich or sparse. Students internalized information as their emerging understandings were verified and clarified. Finally, they contributed clues. The teachers helped students learn within their zones of proximal development.

The second learning principle was the *need to embrace the complexity of the instructional situation*. Scaffolding was not a simple process. It was very complex because students were at varying places in learning. The teachers had to provide varying amounts of scaffolding for some students as they struggled to internalize a new concept, strategy, or disposition. Simultaneously, other students were applying that same new knowledge on their own.

Finally, the study illustrated the important principle of *question and comment generation*. Sternberg (1994) states that children are natural question askers, but that they lose this strategy if adults don't respond appropriately to their questions and comments. Responding appropriately means allowing children to assume responsibility for their own learning, while providing them with explanations, clarifications, and feedback. As their tentative questions and comments are expressed, the students need to learn how to verify and clarify one another's thinking.

The teachers in this study used scaffolding to create opportunities for students to generate questions and comments. They also used the learning conversations as vehicles to respond to those generated questions and answers. Questions and comments were made. Hypotheses were created and tried out. Challenging and supporting occurred. New information was sought, in oral and printed forms. Thoughts were clarified and expanded. The teachers in this study agree with Sternberg's (1994) contention that the single most helpful thing a teacher can do to help children learn is to take their questions and comments seriously and turn those questions and comments into learning opportunities.

Scaffolding is an important instructional tool because it supports students' learning. It helps students to understand that they can teach and learn from others. This leads to collaboration—an important life skill. Students who work together to frame and to solve problems have opportunities to experience this collaboration. Students need practice in order to actively construct knowledge, make connections, and build mental schemata. Learning in this type of socially constructed environment leads students to take responsibility for their own learning and respect their own and others' thinking. Learning conversations provide opportunities for students to verbalize their thoughts. When it comes to collaborative problem-framing and -solving situations, students who learn with the assistance of scaffolding in socially constructed environments will have an advantage over students who do not.

REFERENCES

Bruner, J (1984). Vygotsky's zone of proximal development: The hidden agenda. In B. Rogoff & J. Wertsch (Eds.), *Children's learning in the "zone of proximal development"*. San Francisco: Jossey-Bass.

DiPardo, A., & Freedman, S. (1988). Peer response groups in the writing classroom: Theoretic foundations and new directions. *Review of Educational Research, 58*(2), 119-149.

Doyle, W. (1986). Classroom organization and management. In M.C. Wittrock (Ed.), *Handbook of research on teaching* (3rd ed.). New York: Macmillan.

Duffy, G., & Roehler, L. (1993). *Improving classroom reading instruction: A decision making approach.* New York: McGraw-Hill, Inc.

Duffy, G., Roehler, L., & Herrmann, B. (1988). Modeling mental processes helps poor readers become strategic readers. *The Reading Teacher, 41*(8), 762-767.

Duffy, G., Roehler, L., Meloth, M., & Vavrus, L. (1986). Conceptualizing instructional explanation. *Teaching and Teacher Education, 2*(3), 197-214.

Duffy, G., Roehler, L., & Rackliffe, G. (1986). How teachers' instructional talk influences students' understanding of lesson content. *Elementary School Journal, 87*(1), 3-16.

Fenstermaker, G. (1992). The concepts of method and manner in teaching. In F. Oser, A. Dick, & J. Patry (Eds.), *Effective and responsible teaching: The new synthesis.* San Francisco: Jossey-Bass.

Gallimore, R., & Tharp, R. (1989). Rousing schools to life. *American Educator, 13,* 20-25, 46-52.

Gallimore, R., & Tharp, R. (1990). Teaching mind in society: Teaching, schooling and literate discourse. In L.C. Moll (Ed.), *Vygotsky and education: Instructional implications and applications of sociohistorical psychology.* Cambridge, England: Cambridge University Press.

Gavelek, J. (1986). The social contexts of literacy and schooling: A developmental perspective. In T.E. Raphael (Ed.), *The contexts of school-based literacy.* New York: Random House.

Glaser, B. (1978). *Theoretical sensitivity.* Mill Valley, CA: The Sociology Press.

Glaser, B., & Strauss, A. (1967). *The discovery of grounded theory: Strategies for qualitative research.* Chicago: Aldine.

Goldenberg, C. (1991). Instructional conversation: Promoting comprehension through discussion. *The Reading Teacher, 46,* 316-326.

Gorden, R. (1980). *Interviewing: Strategies, techniques and tactics.* Homewood, IL: Dorsey Press.

Keats, E.J. (1965). *John Henry.* New York: Alfred A. Knopf, Inc.

Kellogg, S. (1986). *Pecos Bill.* New York: Scholastic, Inc.

Lampert, M. (1990). When the problem is not the question and the solution is not the answer: Mathematical knowing thinking. *American Educational Research Journal, 27,* 29-63.

Martin, J. (1985). *Reclaiming a conversation: The ideal of the educated woman.* New

Haven, CT: Yale University Press.

Musser, G., & Burger, W. (1988). *Mathematics for elementary teachers*. New York: Macmillan.

Palincsar, A., Anderson, C., & David, Y. (1993). Pursuing scientific literacy in the middle grades through collaborative problem solving. *The Elementary School Journal, 93*, 643-658.

Paris, S., Lipson, M., & Wixson, K. (1983). Becoming a strategic reader. *Contemporary Educational Psychology, 8*, 293-316.

Pearson, P.D. (1985). Changing the face of reading comprehension instruction. *The Reading Teacher, 38*(8), 724-738.

Raphael, T., Goatley, V., McMahon, S., & Woodman, D. (1995). Promoting meaningful conversations in student book clubs. In N. Roser & M. Martinez (Eds.), *Book talk and beyond: Children and teachers respond to literature*. Newark, DE: International Reading Association.

Roehler, L., & Duffy, G. (1991). Teachers' instructional actions. In R. Barr, M. Kamil, P. Mosenthal, & P.D. Pearson (Eds.), *Handbook of reading research: Volume two*. New York: Longman.

Roehler, L., Hallenback, M., McLellan, M., & Svoboda, N. (1996). Teaching skills through learning conversations in whole language classrooms. In E. McIntyre & M. Pressley (Eds.), *Balanced instruction: Strategies and skills in whole language*. Norwood, MA: Christopher Gordan.

Roehler, L., McLellan, M., & Svoboda, N. (1993). *Developing voice in collaborative classrooms*. Paper presented at the annual meeting of the American Educational Research Association.

Rommetveit, R. (1974). *On message structure: A framework for the study of language and connection*. New York: John Wiley.

San Souci, R.D., & Pinkney, B. (1993). *Cut From the Same Cloth*. New York: Putnam & Grosset Group.

Smagorinsky, P. (1995). The social construction of data: Methodological problems of investigation learning in the zone of proximal development. *Review of Educational Research, 65*(3), 191-212.

Sternberg, R. (1994). Answering questions and questioning answers: Guiding children to intellectual excellence. *Phi Delta Kappan, 76*(2), 136-138.

Vygotsky, L. (1978). *Mind in society: The development of higher psychological processes* (M. Cole, V. John-Steiner, S. Scribner, & E. Souberman, Eds. and Trans.). Cambridge, MA: Harvard University Press.

Wertsch, J. (1985). *Culture, communication, and cognition*. Cambridge, England: Cambridge University Press.

Wertsch, J., McNamee, G., McLare, J., & Budwig, N. (1980). The adult-child dyad as a problem-solving system. *Child Development, 51*, 1215-1221.

Wood, D., Bruner, J., & Ross, G. (1976). The role of tutoring and problem solving. *Journal of Child Psychology and Psychiatry, 17,* 89-100.

CHAPTER TWO

Scaffolding the Development of Intelligence among Children who are Delayed in Learning to Read

IRENE W. GASKINS, SHARON RAUCH, ELEANOR GENSEMER, ELIZABETH CUNICELLI, COLLEEN O'HARA, LINDA SIX, & THERESA SCOTT, Benchmark School

Intelligence is learnable (Perkins, 1995). The job of parents, teachers, and other caretakers is to provide scaffolds that support its development. For some children, each scaffold that is built can be lightly constructed and quickly removed. However, for delayed readers—the ones who most need to acquire the knowledge, strategies, and dispositions that will allow them to think as well as their more successful peers—the scaffolds are often too fragile and of insufficient duration. This chapter deals with ways educators can scaffold the development of intelligent behavior among delayed readers.

Psychologists tend to agree that two basic mechanisms underlie intelligence, a genetically determined *neural intelligence* and an environmentally determined *learned intelligence* (Gardner, 1983; Perkins, 1995; Sternberg, 1990). Neural intelligence is the brain's hard-wiring. It establishes each individual's range of possible mental operations. This range is sufficiently broad for each individual so that functioning at the upper limits is rarely achieved. The basic mechanisms of learned intelligence are the knowledge, strategies, and dispositions that result from and are shaped by experience and reflection. By providing children with the scaffolding, experiences, and time for reflection that each needs to acquire knowledge, strategies, and thinking dispositions, we put children in control of their own intellectual destinies. As a result, these children will have the intelligence to be successful in the areas to which they choose to devote their effort and practice.

Disposition is the part of intelligence shaped by beliefs, values, attitudes, and personal styles; it affects children's will to learn and to employ what they know. Dispositions are the motivational/affective mechanisms that energize and direct how children perceive, generate, and use knowledge and strategies. Two recent books, *Learned Optimism* (Seligman, 1990) and *Emotional Intelligence* (Goleman, 1995), examine the emotional side of intelligence. Both books cite clinical evidence for two propositions: (1) people can modify the cognitive habits that hold them back from performing as intelligently as they might, and (2) important traits for intelligent behavior such as self-awareness, impulse control, persistence, and self-motivation can be learned.

Never before have the ability and the disposition to think well been more important. Success in today's world, both in and out of school, depends on knowing how to think, learn, and problem solve. The shift during the past decade in the United States from an industrial-based economy to a service- and idea-based economy makes it critical that we support our young people in acquiring the knowledge, strategies, and dispositions that promote more intelligent thinking and behavior. We no longer live in a society in which the knowledge and thinking of a few managers assures the success of an organization while the other employees merely follow orders from above. In today's organization, managers know that the success of their enterprise depends on employees who are continually learning and have the personal skills to do so in collaboration with others. Corporations call themselves "learning organizations," underscoring the importance of employees' ability and willingness to learn (Argyris,

1993; Pinchot & Pinchot, 1993; Senge, 1990; Waitley, 1995; Wick & Leon, 1993).

Clearly, in preparing students for success in the twenty-first century, teachers need to keep in mind the importance of students' knowing how to generate and use knowledge—knowledge about content, about strategies, and about dispositions. In the hands of our students, this knowledge can be translated into the power to succeed. It is particularly critical that we provide delayed readers with this power by scaffolding their learning experiences in a way that prepares them to think on a conceptual level commensurate with that of their age-mates.

SCAFFOLDING DEFINED

A scaffold is a support, such as the temporary framework that supports workers during the construction of a building. As it relates to intelligent behavior, scaffolding refers to the supportive situations adults create to help children extend current skills and knowledge to a higher level of competence (Rogoff, 1990). It is support at the edge of a child's competence. In school settings, scaffolding is "what teachers say or do to enable children to complete complex mental tasks they could not complete without assistance" (Pearson & Fielding, 1991, p. 842). The concept of scaffolding was popularized by Bruner (Wood, Bruner, & Ross, 1976) and is grounded in the developmental theories of Vygotsky (1978), who proposed that adult guidance could help children to develop higher psychological functioning. Vygotsky suggested that adult support allows children to operate in the *zone of proximal development*, the area between what a child can accomplish unaided and what that same child can accomplish with assistance. The assistance or instruction proceeds ahead of development, rousing to life functions that are in a stage of maturing (Vygotsky, 1978). In this spirit, Tharp and Gallimore (1988) suggest that teaching should be redefined as assisted performance. Ideally, scaffolding should take place in a convivial, collaborative environment, where children's contributions are accepted as worthy of consideration and where their understanding is frequently assessed. With adult assistance, children internalize knowledge of content, strategies, and thinking dispositions. This knowledge will guide intelligent behavior in similar, future tasks. As the child grows in competence, there is a gradual withdrawal of support, and the child takes on more responsibility for completing the task.

To implement scaffolding successfully, teachers first determine the difference between what each student can accomplish independently and what he or she can accomplish with guidance—the student's zone of proximal development. They then provide instruction with just enough support for the students to participate in tasks that would be beyond their reach without teacher support. Levels of support in scaffolding vary widely. An example of a great deal of support would be when a teacher models the complete performance of a task, with verbal explanations that identify the elements of the content, strategy, and/or thinking disposition. An example of very little support would be when a teacher simply cues some aspect of the task in response to what students have already mastered. Levels of support between these two extremes include *assisted modeling*, in which students are encouraged to participate in the completion of the task; *element identification*, in which the teacher identifies the elements of the intelligent behavior as the student completes the task; and *strategy naming*, in which the teacher refers to the name of the strategy and students then employ it on their own (Beed, Hawkins, & Roller, 1991).

When students independently attempt tasks that previously were scaffolded, they hear the adult's questions and guidance in their minds directing them through the task. The teacher's voice becomes the students' self-directing speech. Students complete the formerly scaffolded task through conscious self-regulation of knowledge, strategies, and dispositions. Generally, with practice, they eventually complete similar tasks automatically. They no longer need direction from the adult or from themselves. As a result of the automaticity and situational knowledge they have built up through practice and experience, they just *do* it, with a minimum of reflection. At this point, students have moved from the zone of proximal development into the developmental stage for that task. However, it is not uncommon for de-automatization to occur, requiring a trip back through the zone of proximal development to regain their understanding and perform at a satisfactory level.

In summary, scaffolding means explaining, demonstrating, and jointly constructing an idealized version of a performance. Scaffolding includes recruiting the student's interest, reducing the number of steps so the task is manageable, maintaining students' persistence toward the goal, making critical features evident, and controlling frustration and risk. Such instruction has been variously called *assisted performance* (Tharp & Gallimore, 1988), *responsive teaching* (Gaskins, Anderson, Pressley, Cunicelli, & Satlow, 1993), and *cognitive apprenticeship* (Brown, Collins, & Dugiud, 1989; Rogoff, 1990). Tharp and Gallimore (1988) sum up the importance of scaffolding:

> Students cannot be left to learn on their own; teachers cannot be content to provide opportunities to learn and then assess outcomes; recitation must be deemphasized; responsive, assisting interactions must become commonplace in the classroom. Minds must be roused to life (p. 21).

Delayed Readers, Strategies Instruction, and the Benchmark Model

Delayed readers are those children who are unable to read on a level commensurate with that of their successful age-mates, despite having average or above-average intelligence, the same learning opportunities as the successful readers, and no evidence of primary emotional or neurological problems. These are the children we teach at Benchmark School, a school for 175 delayed readers in grades 1 through 8.

At Benchmark, teachers employ *transactional strategies instruction* (Pressley, El Dinary, Gaskins, Schuder, Bergman, Almasi, & Brown, 1992) to explain and scaffold the strategies that enable students to control the knowledge and dispositions leading to intelligent think-ing and behavior. Strategies instruction is characterized by use of eight instructional moves (Gaskins & Elliot, 1991; Gaskins et al., 1993). Teachers explain *what* strategy students will be learning, *why* it is important, *when* it can be used, and *how* to implement it. They frequently *model* how to implement the strategy in authentic situa-tions, using mental modeling—sharing their thought processes by thinking aloud as they implement the strategy (Duffy, Roehler, & Herrmann, 1988). They also may share a personal experience about how the strategy facilitated intelligent thinking or behavior. Teachers next provide students with *assisted practice*, interacting with the students to scaffold the application of the strategy as they complete one of their school assignments. Gradually, teachers *release responsi-bility* for the strategy as students take on more responsibility for applying the strategy on their own. *Cueing the use of each strategy* is ongoing as students move toward independence in orchestrating strategies during their years at Benchmark. This model of instruction is embedded in a rich literacy environment where children spend a substantial portion of their school day engaged in reading and writing interrelated texts.

The prominent use of scaffolding in Benchmark classrooms, where children advance daily in competence, is based on our aware-ness that most people do not learn intelligent thinking and behavior on their own. Rather, they learn with the help of someone standing by and supporting the struggle. These helpers or mediators offer tips for assessing and thinking about the task at hand. They may, for example, direct learners' attention to important features, pose ques-tions, or suggest what to attend to next. In other cases, they ask what students think they should do, prompt students to ponder what strategy to use, ask why students think a possible answer is right or wrong, draw the students' attention to inconsistencies, or encourage students to check the completeness or accuracy of an answer or idea. These transactions are most profitable when teachers are helping students solve authentic problems that arise throughout the school day. Modeling, coaching, and fading of support are used to approach real learning problems that occur when students need and want to complete real tasks. As a result of the teacher's skillful scaffolding, students participate in the entire process of completing the task even before they can carry it out independently. Scaffolding makes a dramatic difference in the complexity of the tasks learners can attempt and their success with these tasks (Perkins, 1995). In addition, students internalize the mediator's questions and prompts and form the mental habit of attending to them. When this happens, students have become not only self-mediating, but more intelligent.

This chapter will focus on scaffolding in the form of assisted practice and cueing. Scaffolding will be discussed as a transition from teacher modeling and control to student control. The remainder of the chapter will describe how the Benchmark School staff scaffolds the development of three components of intelligent behavior. The first component is knowledge—knowledge of content, knowledge of strategies that complement how the brain works, and knowledge of personal styles and dispositions. A second component is putting what one knows to good use—the application of cognitive and metacognitive strategies. The third component is the affective-style component—the regulation of dispositions, such as the dispositions to be attentive, actively engaged, reflective, adaptable, and persistent.

SCAFFOLDING IN ACTION

The process of scaffolding, as described earlier, is the same whether we are teaching first-year Benchmark students or more experienced students. However, instructional objectives are often more discrete for those just entering Benchmark and more integrated for students who have been at the school for a number of years. For example, a lesson for beginning students may focus on a disposition, such as *reflectivity*, with the stated goal: "to *take time* to listen to, and understand, all the directions before beginning a task." With more advanced students, it is common to scaffold the integration of all three aspects of intelligence—knowledge, strategies, and disposition—

while explaining one aspect explicitly as the specific objective of the lesson.

Decisions about how quickly to move through the process of scaffolding are based on the teacher's goals and the students' responses. The steps may be recursive or linear, depending on the situation. As teachers make minute-by-minute decisions about the level of scaffolding to provide, they are asking themselves questions such as: How does this move the students closer to the goal? How can I take this response and use it to make the students more aware of the process they are using?

Tharp and Gallimore (1988) suggest six ways teachers might assist performance in the zone of proximal development. These include *modeling, contingency managing, feeding back, instructing, questioning,* and *cognitive structuring.* In the Benchmark model, some of these methods are recurrences of instructional moves that have been used earlier, but are repeated as needed during assisted practice. Other methods of assisting occur for the first time during guided practice. Quite often, several methods of assisting occur in one scaffolded interaction. The following section discusses examples of ways the Benchmark School staff scaffolds the development of intelligent thinking and behavior.

Content Knowledge

One teacher's year-long objective for her first-grade mathematics class was that math must make sense. An organizing principle of mathematics that enables students to make sense of numbers and number relationships is *recognizing and building patterns.* Prior to the lesson described here, students collected examples of patterns from magazines and built patterns using pattern blocks. They also learned how to skip-count by 2, 5, and 10. Knowledge of skip-counting by ten provided the knowledge base for scaffolding the construction of patterns. The teacher initially scaffolded the task by modeling the complete task of recognizing and building patterns.

TEACHER: Today, we are going to build numbers using what we know about patterns. I'm using my definition of patterns and thinking about what I already know. I think I know a number pattern already. *(Writes on the chalkboard: 10, 20, 30, 40, 50.)*

Hmmm. Why do I think this is a pattern? It looks like if I add 10 to the first number, I'll get 20. If I add 10 to 20, I'll get 30. I know that a pattern is something that happens over and over, so I'm thinking, "If I'm adding 10 each time, I must have a pattern." That's the kind of thinking I'd like you to do. Think about what you already know about patterns, such as a pattern repeats over and over, and look for situations where you see that happening. Each one of you has some chips on your desk. I am going to use the overhead projector and my chips to start the pattern.

(Puts up 1 chip.) Can anyone tell me the pattern?

(At this point the teacher moves from complete modeling to the assisted modeling level of scaffolding by asking questions. These questions guide students to recognize the steps of the thinking process and help them apply knowledge of patterns to new situations.)

STUDENT: You need to add more chips to see a pattern.

TEACHER: So, you think you need more information. Why?

STUDENT: Because a pattern means the same thing happens over again— like with blocks. The blocks were in a certain order and we couldn't know what to do next if we didn't know the pattern.

TEACHER: That's a good explanation, Susan. You are using what you know about patterns. **(The teacher identifies the element of applying the knowledge of patterns to a new situation.)**

(Puts up more chips.) Now, do I have enough information?

STUDENT: Yes, it looks like a +1 pattern.

(Using chips, the students make configurations of the numbers 1 through 5 on their desk using the +1 pattern.)

Whenever necessary, the teacher assists students in applying their understanding of how a pattern works in this new situation.

TEACHER: I'm impressed because you used what you know about patterns—that a pattern repeats over and over again. Now I have a really difficult question for you. (**The teacher gives specific feedback and sets students up to take more responsibility for applying the knowledge of patterns to a new situation.**)

(Puts entire pattern on the overhead.)

TEACHER: What groups would I take away if I wanted to show a +2 pattern? Think carefully before you answer. What do you need to think about first? (**The teacher breaks the task into parts by asking specific questions that a child can repeat to him/herself to complete similar tasks.**)

STUDENT: What +2 means.

TEACHER: What does +2 mean?

STUDENT: Add +2 over and over again.

STUDENT: Add 2 to the first number, then 2 to the second number and on and on.

TEACHER: Check your work. Make sure you ask yourself if the number you added to your pattern makes sense. Does it follow the pattern? (**The teacher encourages self-monitoring.**) Who wants to tell me what your new pattern looks like?

STUDENT: I took away 1 and 3 and 5 and I added 6 because when you count by 2's you say 2, 4, 6, 8. Each time I added 2 chips.

TEACHER: Thanks, Andy. Does anyone have anything different?

The teacher continued in this vein, guiding students to observe the +2 pattern as it relates to odd numbers. This exercise, adding 2 to even and odd numbers, continued with scaffolding until the students were able to recognize the +2 pattern with a variety of two- and three-digit numbers.

Another example of the construction of content knowledge occurred in a middle-school language arts class, a class that students often believe has no content. The teacher's goal for this series of lessons was to make students conscious of the important role content plays in constructing meaning from a novel, especially historical fiction. She wanted students to regard building background knowledge as an important strategy for understanding challenging historical fiction. In previous lessons, the students had determined that the strategies they used in social studies—such as assessing what they already knew about the important events of an historical period and filling in the gaps from the text to be read—might work in language arts, too. They had already done research to build background knowledge relevant to the setting—pre-revolutionary Boston—of the next novel they would read. In addition, from their background knowledge of the historical fiction genre, and through previous reading of *My Brother Sam Is Dead* (Collier & Collier, 1974), the students were aware that reading fiction set in a particular time period could teach them about that period's everyday culture. Now that they had acquired content knowledge about the time period, they were about to read the more challenging *Johnny Tremain* (Forbes, 1971).

Writing in a learning log as they connected ideas and learned historical content helped scaffold students' thinking. The questions that students answered in their learning logs were intended to help them understand the content of their reading and, more importantly, to give them a generic framework for interpreting historical fiction. The questions used were:

(a)   What were the major events described?
(b)   What aspects of the culture were described?
(c)   How did the major events change the culture?

At the time of the scaffolding example below, students had just read one chapter and responded in their learning log. They were now meeting to discuss and add to their knowledge by making their learning logs as complete as possible. Since they were being led through the process of selecting information from their background knowledge and applying it to understand new information, the teacher was using a scaffolding method in which students are guided to reflect on elements of the understandings being developed.

TEACHER: Now that we've discussed what happened in this chapter, let's answer the first question in your learning log, about how the major events may have changed the way the people of Boston lived. What major events were described in this chapter? (**In an attempt to guide the students toward the use of a generic framework, the teacher always presents the questions in the a-b-c order listed above.**)

STUDENT: The Boston Tea Party was the most important. The author spent a lot of time on that. I thought it was neat. Why did they clean up when they were done?

TEACHER: Does anyone have an idea about that? (**Whenever possible with students reading at this advanced level, the teacher will serve as a mediator, rather than answer the students' questions directly.**)

STUDENT: They didn't want people to think they were stealing or just messing around. The "Indians" were making a point.

(The group discussion moved to the next section of the learning log.)

TEACHER: What aspects of the culture were described in this section?

STUDENT: Communication—they only had posters, and word of mouth, and sometimes newspapers.

TEACHER: Good. Keep that in mind. Anything else? (**The teacher is cueing students that this information will be important to consider later in the discussion. This refocuses the discussion to the generic questions.**)

STUDENT: Well, tea must have been important if they thought it was such a sacrifice to dump it.

STUDENT: Yeah, and what will Parliament do to them?

TEACHER: You're certainly asking yourselves an important question. Consequences of any action are important to consider as part of a culture.

(After further discussion of aspects of the culture that were described in the chapter, the teacher moved on to the third point, which is how the big events changed the culture.)

TEACHER: Has anything changed for the people of Boston because of the Tea Party?

STUDENT: Because of the boycotts and now the dumping of the tea, people aren't living so well. Food is scarce or not as good ...

STUDENT: And people really hate each other, and there are lots of rumors because communication isn't good. I can predict that England will be really mad at the colonists and do something drastic.

TEACHER: What have you just done in order to make these logical predictions about how Parliament might treat the people of Boston?

STUDENT: I thought about how daily life is changing because of the colonists' protest.

TEACHER: Yes, you connected ideas from your knowledge of important events and daily life with what the author is saying. You did this to make predictions that keep you involved and help you focus on the important information. (**By identifying elements of the process, the teacher is attempting to make the students more aware of the thinking process they have just used.**)

The teacher would expect students to use the generic questions more independently to integrate ideas as they read other historical fiction books. The questions should become the voices heard in students' heads to enable them to scaffold their own learning from historical fiction at some future date. The strategy to develop background knowledge before reading the novel, as well as the generic questions, scaffolded the interpretation of the novel. As a result, students will have a more intelligent means of approaching historical fiction in the future.

Strategies

Teachers scaffold knowledge of strategies in many ways. At the assisted modeling level of scaffolding, a third-grade teacher alerted students to the fact that that day's science reading might include some multisyllabic words that they had not seen in print before. With these young students, the teacher provided a great deal of assistance by doing more modeling and asking more specific questions than teachers would do with students reading at a higher level. Prior to the excerpt cited below, the teacher had pointed out that the words were well defined in the text and had been discussed in class, but might seem at first glance to have too many letters to be decoded easily. The teacher scaffolded the students' approach to these words by modeling how she would decode a multisyllabic word. First, she cued the students to access their background knowledge of word identification strategies and to think about what they already knew about spelling patterns. She then modeled the application of this knowledge to a specific word. At various points in the process, she elicited students' assistance to demonstrate how the knowledge they already had could be transferred to this new situation.

TEACHER: You are telling me that when I come to a "college" word like the one I have written on the chalkboard, I should look for spelling patterns, then use words I know with the same spelling patterns to figure out how to pronounce each chunk. Let's see if that works. *(Points to TRANSLUCENT on the chalkboard, which is written in the sentence: "Water is translucent.")*

Hmmm. Two of the words I see in the sentence are words I just know. However, that long word isn't one I just know, so I will have to decode it. Rather than match a sound to each letter—which is inefficient now that we have begun to see patterns in words—I will look at each letter from the beginning to the end and see if there are chunks that I know. I know that more mature readers look for patterns in words. Let's see, I see a blend, there's a vowel, a lot of consonants, another vowel, a consonant, another vowel, and then a couple of consonants. *(Points to each part of the word that she mentions.)* Anyone have any idea how many chunks I should divide this word into to figure it out? (**The teacher cues students to think of the first step in decoding a multisyllabic word—the need to divide the word into parts for ease in decoding it. In addition, she is assessing the students' level of independence in applying chunking skills associated with decoding multisyllabic words.**)

STUDENT: There are probably three chunks because there are three vowels all by themselves and that means three spelling patterns.

TEACHER: Great, you remembered the first step in decoding a multisyllabic word—divide the word into as many chunks as there are vowels that we expect to hear. Okay, let's see if that works—three vowels and three chunks. Do you recognize any chunks with common patterns? (**The teacher again states a step students might use. As a result of this scaffolding, the teacher's words may become the voice playing in students' heads when they are decoding a multisyllabic word independently.**)

STUDENT: I see T-R-A-N-S. That is a chunk I see in lots of words like *transportation*.

TEACHER: Yes, we already know other words that begin the same way the word we are decoding does. *Transportation, transfer, translate* are familiar words. (**The teacher uses mental modeling to share her thought processes about common morphemes.**) Sometimes "college" words have common endings, too. I think I will look at the last vowel and see if I recognize a spelling pattern. That C-E-N-T looks familiar. I know the word TENT, so I think the ending says CENT. Other words I know end with that pattern, like *recent* and *magnificent*. I think that will be the end chunk. Now I just have the middle chunk, L-U, left. Here I have a U hanging off the end of a chunk. Anyone know what we can do with that? (**With this question, the teacher moves from totally modeling the processes to assisted modeling—a good technique for keeping students actively involved in the learning process.**)

STUDENT: I know that when there is a vowel at the end of a chunk, the vowel says its own name—like in *station*.

TEACHER: *(Writes station on the chalkboard with a space between the two syllables—sta tion.)* What do the rest of you think? Any other ideas? (**By not accepting the first student's suggestion as the only possibility, the teacher is being responsive rather than evaluating the student's response.**)

STUDENT: The middle chunk will be LUH, like the sound you hear in chunks that are not stressed, like the sound for E in the middle of *elephant*.

TEACHER: That's a possibility, it could be TRANS LUH CENT. Are there any other possibilities? (**The teacher provides students with a generic question—"Are there other possibilities?"—that should eventually become the voice in their heads when they decode a word that sounds unfamiliar.**)

STUDENT: I think it's LOO because the spelling pattern is the same as the key word FLU.

(**In her next response, the teacher prepares students for the element identification level of scaffolding by identifying the elements of the intelligent behavior that led the students to be able to decode this word.**)

TEACHER: You've told me a lot about how to decode this word. You told me to break it into manageable chunks, and you told me how many chunks make up the word based on the number of vowels sounds. Next, you looked for familiar patterns and you recognized morphemes you knew at the beginning and at the end of the word. Finally you were flexible and suggested several ways to pronounce the word. Let's see if I can put the chunks together. It could be TRANS LUH CENT or it could be TRANS LOO CENT. Let me check it in the sentence. The water is TRANS LUH CENT. I don't know that word. The water is TRANS LOO CENT. Oh, *translucent*, I know that's a real word. I've heard *translucent* before. Can anyone tell me what it means?

In similar situations in the future, the teacher might simply cue the students, reminding them to apply the three steps: to break the word into chunks; to look for common patterns; and to be flexible and try several possible pronunciations.

Another example of scaffolding the application of a strategy comes from a class of more advanced students. Although this lesson (like the other examples above) contains elements of knowledge, strategies, and dispositions, the lesson had a strategy focus. The goal for second- and third-year middle-school science students is to develop a plan for learning science which they can take with them to any other science classroom. The lesson contains elements of four levels of scaffolding: *complete modeling, assisted modeling, element identification*, and *strategy naming*. Scaffolding of strategies in science begins the first day of school, when students learn that the final project for the year is a performance-based assessment that requires them to construct and use a personal plan for learning science. Students select a socially relevant and controversial topic, research the topic, write a formal research paper, compile a portfolio of their research and their thinking, take some action in connection with their issue, and present their findings at a science symposium during the last week of school. A basic research plan is used continuously throughout the year, with responsibility released to students as they are ready to assume that responsibility for themselves. At the beginning of the year, each element of the basic research plan is completely scaffolded for the students. As control of applying the strategies shifts from the teacher to the students during the course of the year, the scaffolding moves through different levels of support to accommodate the students' changing needs.

Search is one of the important elements of the research plan. The search process includes brainstorming to access background knowledge, searching easy-reading texts to learn the vocabulary connected to the topic being studied, applying strategies for recording and organizing information, and evaluating knowledge through problem solving in real-life situations. The lesson below occurred during the first month of school. The objectives of the lesson were to guide students to discover the value of easy reading as an element in the search process, and to adapt the note-taking strategy they had learned in social studies class to their note-taking needs for the science project. The teacher began the lesson with these advanced middle-school students by reviewing the elements of intelligent behavior they had already used. She then assessed their knowledge of the search process by posing two questions that are generic to the search process. These questions will become the voices in their heads as the year progresses.

TEACHER: We've discussed our content objective—to understand weather and how it affects our lives. We've done some brainstorming to activate background knowledge, and now we need to begin to gather information. What is the first thing we do to begin our search? What do we need to know first?

STUDENT: We need to know what weather is.

STUDENT: We need to know some of the vocabulary that goes with weather.

TEACHER: What is the most efficient way for us to get that information?

STUDENT: Easy reading—reading books that will give us the vocabulary and the definitions in a way that we can understand.

(The teacher begins by modeling her own behavior in a similar situation.)

TEACHER: I agree. When I do research reports for my graduate school classes, I know that first I must understand the words that go with a topic, then I can more easily understand the hard information. Thus, I go to the juvenile section of the library first. I want the important vocabulary in the fastest, easiest way available to me, and I often can get that information from children's or young adult books. So our strategy is to use easy reading as a way to get information about the vocabulary that is part of our topic of weather. We can do this any time we begin to search or learn about a new topic. We know from our discussions in Psych 102 *[a course in which middle-school students are taught how the mind works]* that we need to learn and use information rather than just memorize it, and so by beginning with basic definitions, we have a framework in our heads onto which we can hook new information. Those key words and definitions from easy reading can be the framework to which we hook new information later in our search. We have several easy-reading books, but if the information from those books is going to be useful in our search, we need some way to keep track of it. What would you suggest? **(With this question the teacher begins the assisted modeling level of scaffolding.)**

STUDENT: We need to take notes.

STUDENT: We should look for important words in the easy reading books.

STUDENT: We could use the note-taking strategy we learned in social studies.

TEACHER: Okay, so we need a method for note taking that will allow us to focus on the vocabulary and the explanations of those important words. Can we use the same strategy you use in social studies? What are the steps you use for that strategy? (**The teacher uses this question to lead the students to identify the elements of the strategy. Since these are more advanced students, they, rather than the teacher, have responsibility for identifying these elements.**)

STUDENT: Survey to figure out what the book is about and to decide if it will help us get the information we need about weather.

STUDENT: Read carefully to find out what the main ideas are. We use the main ideas to set purposes for reading.

TEACHER: Why do we set purposes for reading?

STUDENT: To keep us involved in what we read.

STUDENT: To help us sort out what is important in the book, and what is interesting but not useful. We keep track of the important information that helps answer our purpose questions.

STUDENT: To record important information in an organized way. Information to answer each purpose question is written under the question.

TEACHER: After we set purposes for reading, what is next?

STUDENT: Reread the material to take the notes.

STUDENT: In social studies we write the purpose questions on notebook paper and take notes under each question.

TEACHER: Those are all excellent suggestions for note taking, and it sounds as if that process works in social studies. Information in science books is organized a little differently, and our purpose for reading these easy science books is a bit different from your purposes for reading in social studies, so I have designed a note-taking sheet for taking notes in science class. Let's take a look at it. It has three columns—a column for key words, a column for explanations or information from the text or diagrams of the concepts, and a column for questions that we have about the vocabulary or the concepts we read about. Does this note-taking sheet accomplish the same thing as the note-taking step in the social studies process?

STUDENT: It does. It's just a different way to record the information. It seems weird to do it this way instead of just on a piece of paper.

TEACHER: What are the advantages to using a format like this when we are reading an easy-reading book?

STUDENT: You can see the key vocabulary words because they are in a separate column.

STUDENT: In social studies we don't write down questions that we have. We write down important information from the book.

TEACHER: You're right. This part of the note-taking process is different than the format you use in social studies because it helps to highlight the important vocabulary we need to identify at this early stage in our search, and it gives us an opportunity to generate questions that we think about as we are doing the easy reading. Let's experiment with this different format for recording notes as we go through the first easy-reading book together.

Students independently worked through the steps that were similar to the note-taking strategy they use in social studies. They surveyed the book, read carefully, and set purposes for reading. A whole-class discussion, facilitated by the teacher, helped the group settle on purpose questions related to defining weather and the characteristics of weather. The teacher then read the easy-reading book, modeled the thinking process involved in selecting the key words, and modeled recording those key words and explanations on the note-taking sheet. At the end of the first easy-reading book, the class discussed the process and reflected on the usefulness of the new strategy. Modeling, guided practice, and element identification con-tinued with several other easy-reading books until students were ready to assume responsibility for using the adapted note-taking strategy with easy-reading text. After a period of time, as the students became more independent, the teacher moved to the strategy-naming level of scaffolding.

TEACHER: We're now ready to focus our study of weather on a particular aspect of weather. We're going to take a look at storms. We have an easy-reading book on storms. What should we do with this book? (This question leads the students to identify the steps in the process they would use. The teacher names the strategy they have described, and reminds them of other situations in which it will be useful. This represents an advanced state of scaffolding in which students are close to moving from the zone of proximal development to their developmental level.)

Dispositions

Scaffolded instruction is used not only to foster the development of content and strategies, but also to help students modify aspects of their personal style that interfere with learning. What follows is an example from a math class.

Students at an early elementary level do not seem to be aware of the thinking dispositions that must undergird mathematical thinking. Thus, we attempt to develop this awareness and to guide students in developing the dispositions of mathematical thinkers and problem solvers. Younger Benchmark students are familiar with the phrase *mathematical thinker*, but often have difficulty adapting their individual styles to follow mathematical thinking steps without teacher cueing. In the following lesson, the teacher reviews some aspects of the thinking disposition of a mathematical thinker, guides students to identify the elements of this thinking disposition, and models a personal example of reflective thinking. The teacher begins the lesson by guiding her seven- and eight-year-olds to identify the dispositional elements of intelligent mathematical behavior. These dispositional characteristics are basic to students successfully carrying out Polya's (1957) four-step problem-solving strategy: *understand the problem, plan, solve,* and *check.*

TEACHER: Who can tell me what you need to do to be Student of the Day?
STUDENT: Pay attention.
TEACHER: What does that mean?
STUDENT: Sit up straight, don't fiddle around, keep your eyes on the speaker, and participate.

TEACHER: Yes, these are all things that good students do! To understand what to do, you need to tune in to what is being taught. Looking at the speaker and participating keep you tuned in. What is a second thing you might do to earn Student of the Day?

STUDENT: Be a mathematical thinker.

TEACHER: That sounds hard to do. Pretend I am a visitor to your class and tell me what that means.

STUDENT: It is the way mathematicians think. That means they are reflective.

TEACHER: Well, what can I do to be reflective?

STUDENT: You have to think about what the teacher is asking you to do and you have to think about the strategies you should use to get your work done and you have to check your answer.

TEACHER: Anything else?

STUDENT: First, before you do anything you have to stop. You stop and take time to think. I mean you shouldn't raise your hand and answer without thinking about what you want to say first.

Next, the teacher reviews the dispositional characteristics of the mathematical thinking process that she would like them to use, then models how she might employ these characteristics.

TEACHER: So, in order to be a mathematical thinker, I have to be reflective. That means I take time to think, to understand the problem, and to find a strategy that will help me solve the problem. Then, I have to check my answer. Well, I did that yesterday when the custodian asked me to help him with a problem. He said that he had set up 15 chairs in one of the conference rooms, but Dr. Gaskins told him he only needed to have 9. He wanted to know how many to take away. I had to think a minute because I didn't have my calculator with me and I had to come up with a strategy that would help me solve this problem. So I said to myself, "I know that 15 minus 10 is 5 and 10 is one more than 9. So, I should take away 5 chairs plus 1, which would be 6. The custodian was happy that I was able to give him the answer. I was happy that I had been reflective and that I was thinking like a mathematician.

The teacher uses a generic question to begin the assisted modeling level of scaffolding and breaks the task into manageable chunks.

TEACHER: Now let's practice being reflective mathematical thinkers. If the answer is 11, what is the problem? What's the first thing I have to do to figure this out?

STUDENT: I have to take time to be sure that I understand what I'm supposed to do.

TEACHER: Yes, taking time to think is the key to becoming a good mathematical thinker.

STUDENT: I have to make up an addition problem whose answer is 11.

STUDENT: It can be either addition or subtraction. Right?

TEACHER: Will both operations give you an answer of 11? (**Notice that the teacher does not simply tell the student the answer. Rather, she provides him with a question he can ask himself to solve his own dilemma.**)

STUDENT: Yes.

TEACHER: You may use whichever operation will give you 11. What is the next thing you have to think about?

STUDENT: I have to think of a strategy to help me solve this problem.

TEACHER: I want you all to take a few minutes to work on this.

(Students work on problem.)

OK. Who's ready?

STUDENT: I knew I had to use addition or subtraction to find a problem whose answer is 11. I decided to use addition. I know that 11 is one more than 10 and I know a doubles fact for ten—5 + 5 = 10. So if 11 is one more than ten, I can use doubles plus one. 5 + 6 = 11. I checked my answer by counting on. The problem is: What is 5 + 6?

TEACHER: Did anyone think about this differently?

STUDENT: Yes. I decided to find a subtraction problem whose answer is 11. I wanted my problem to have an 8 in it, so I used the counting-

> on strategy. I said 9, 10, 11. That's 3 more. So, 11 − 8 = 3. I checked it because I know that 11 − 8 = 3 is a turnaround fact for 8 + 3 = 11. My problem is 11 − 8 = 3.
>
> TEACHER: To be a mathematical thinker, you have to be reflective. You didn't rush to solve the problem. You followed all the steps for thinking like a mathematician. You took time to understand the problem; you made sure you understood the problem; you found a strategy; and you checked your work. Being reflective took a little longer than writing down the first answer that popped into your head, but taking time to go through the process allowed you to learn a process that you can use for more sophisticated problems. Now we are ready to work with some harder numbers.

After the teacher summarized by identifying how the students exhibited the disposition of a reflective thinker, the students were prepared to apply their understanding of the benefits of taking time to think, as well as the strategies to employ during that thinking time, to a more complex task.

Another example of scaffolding the development of a disposition occurred in a class of older students who had been attending Benchmark for three or four years. A lesson taught early in the year focused on personal style and ways to take charge of style when it presents a roadblock to learning. In previous lessons, students had determined criteria to evaluate the quality of their reading, thought about possible personal-style roadblocks to reading with understanding, and generated strategies to overcome or cope with these roadblocks. Now these processes would be applied to evaluating the quality of the group's discussions. The goal was for students to become aware of, and take charge of, their dispositional roadblocks so that discussions would be as productive as possible. Since it can be difficult for middle-school students to discuss their own needs, the teacher kept the discussion about style issues as impersonal as possible until trust could be established. In this example, the teacher scaffolds the discussion by asking students to identify the elements of intelligent behavior that relate to a good discussion. The teacher's goals are for students to understand the elements of a good discussion; understand how a good discussion can benefit them as learners; and identify, understand, and control their dispositional roadblocks so that they can be effective participants in a discussion.

TEACHER: We've said in earlier lessons that one way to evaluate how well you read and understood is to think about whether the discussion is going well. Lauren, what's one way you can tell that the discussion is going well for you?

STUDENT: If I know what's going on ... If I have something to say about the questions you ask.

TEACHER: So, one way we can tell we're having a good discussion is that the information coming out of the discussion is familiar or makes sense given what was read. What else?

STUDENT: If I was confused, someone clarified the information for me. Then it made sense. Sometimes I got additional information, too.

TEACHER: Interesting—so is it necessarily the teacher who explains?

STUDENT: No, in fact, the less the teacher talks and the more the students talk the better the discussion.

TEACHER: Wow! That's true. If you guys keep the discussion focused and moving, I might not say a word!

(The teacher lists criteria suggested by the students on the chalkboard, criteria that will later be transferred to reference sheets for the students. These criteria will scaffold intelligent behavior in future discussions.)

TEACHER: Now that we know some ways to evaluate a discussion, let's think of some possible roadblocks that might interfere with a good discussion. Can you think of a roadblock to a good discussion? **(The teacher guides and encourages the students to think in terms of behaviors or thinking processes that could interfere. At this point, she is not asking students to necessarily deal with their own dispositions or styles. Students suggest such roadblocks as boredom, poor attention, not understanding the reading, disruptive behavior, noise in the room.)**

TEACHER: I agree. These all could be roadblocks. We may even think of more later. How would you advise a classmate to deal with "being bored" or having a tough time paying attention?

STUDENT: I'd tell him to set a goal to participate a certain number of times. You have to pay attention to participate.

STUDENT: I'd tell him to ask questions so maybe he could feel a part of things.

STUDENT: Sometimes it even helps to do the things we were taught in the lower school like, "keep your eyes on the speaker," or remind yourself of what you learned in Psych 102 *[a course in which students are taught how the mind works]*. You have to believe you can get involved.

TEACHER: These seem like helpful strategies. Are you in big trouble if you didn't understand everything that happened in the chapter?

STUDENT: No way! You can ask for clarification.

STUDENT: You can listen and start connecting ideas with what you already know.
(Students continue to discuss strategies to deal with dispositional or style roadblocks.)

TEACHER: This is a good start in evaluating a discussion and in finding strategies to overcome possible difficulties or roadblocks. Why do you think I was pleased with the discussion we just had?
(Students briefly evaluate the discussion based on their own interest, attention, and participation.)

After several weeks, most students had developed enough trust and confidence to begin referring to their own dispositional roadblocks as they dealt with the three parts of language arts—reading, writing, and discussion. The teacher already had each student's needs in mind and was watching for opportunities to guide each student to recognize his or her needs. What follows is an example of how the teacher assisted Nicole in understanding her personal style. The emphasis here has shifted from teacher modeling to student sharing of what works.

TEACHER: I'm noticing that, instead of being passive, lots of people are taking control of their learning. Nicole, would you be willing to share what happened when you called me over while you were reading?

STUDENT: Sure. I couldn't understand this description on page 104. I tried summarizing in my head, but I couldn't figure it out. I read it again and tried to picture it, but it was no use.

TEACHER: The author does tricky things with description. Did anyone else think that? Andy?

STUDENT: He describes things, but doesn't say what they are. It's like a puzzle you have to figure out. Nicole, remember when he described Beanpole's glasses? You had to figure out what they were and label them.

STUDENT: That's what the teacher reminded me. I needed to think about whether the author had done this before and try to access my background knowledge.

TEACHER: Nicole, that's just what you did. And what did you realize the author was describing?

STUDENT: A grenade!

TEACHER: That's it. Nicole, you used a bunch of good strategies here. What did you do?

STUDENT: Well, first I knew I was missing important information. Then I asked you for clarification.

TEACHER: Did I tell you?

STUDENT: No, you helped me think of what I already knew so I could help myself.

(Following the student sharing, the teacher summarizes by naming the strategies Nicole used.)

TEACHER: Good! Nicole used lots of strategies here and she demonstrated one of the dispositions of intelligent behavior. She was active instead of passive. She took charge of her learning. She did this by using the strategies of summarizing and picturing to monitor her understanding. Did anyone else use similar strategies to take charge of understanding these tricky passages? That's exactly what we all need to do to be independent learners.

Later, when the teacher met with Nicole for a goal-setting conference, she referred back to the reading-group interaction. At this point the teacher is aware that Nicole is becoming more independent in recognizing her dispositional roadblock—the tendency to be passive—and that Nicole is using strategies to overcome this road-block. This is an indication to the teacher that some scaffolding can be removed to enable Nicole to function more independently. The teacher will now help Nicole determine a plan that she can use as she becomes more automatic at taking control of her learning.

TEACHER: Nicole, you did a good job understanding your learning needs in reading group today when you talked about the strategies you used to take charge of understanding what you read. You used several strategies successfully and using them seemed to clarify your thinking. First of all, what was the roadblock you overcame?

STUDENT: I got confused. Sometimes I don't get what is going on and I don't do anything about it.

TEACHER: Okay. What can you do if you are confused and can no longer connect the ideas?

STUDENT: I can ask.

TEACHER: Would you do that first?

STUDENT: No. I can reread and think about how what I am reading fits with what I already know. I want to see if I have strategies to use on my own and use asking for clarification only if I still need help.

TEACHER: Now, let's see how you want to phrase your goal.

STUDENT: I'll take charge of making sense of what I'm reading. I'll monitor my understanding by summarizing in my head. If I get confused, I'll reread, access my background knowledge, or ask for clarifica-tion.

TEACHER: You certainly did that today! Let's write that on your goal sheet. Tomorrow, let's get together and evaluate how effective these strategies are for putting you in charge of your personal style and helping you understand what you read.

In a similar way the teacher would guide students to reflect on their needs until they demonstrate that they can analyze their personal styles independently. The teacher will continue to meet briefly with Nicole each day to assess her progress in overcoming the disposition to be passive and to help her evaluate the effectiveness of her plan.

CONCLUDING THOUGHTS

One of the rewarding and challenging aspects of being a teacher is knowing that under our guidance children can learn to be more intelligent. For this to happen, we must assist students in the development of the elements of intelligent behavior. Teachers need to recognize each student's level of competence with respect to content knowledge, strategies, and control over dispositions, then scaffold the development of each in a way that moves students toward the goal of behaving and thinking intelligently.

Scaffolding refers to the supportive situations adults create in which children can extend current knowledge, strategies, and dispositions to a higher level of competence. Scaffolding entails explaining, demonstrating, and jointly constructing an idealized version of a performance. It includes recruiting the student's interest, reducing the number of steps so a task is manageable, maintaining students' persistence toward the goal, making critical features evident, and controlling frustration and risk. The process of scaffolding is the same whether we are teaching first-year students or more experienced students, and is applicable across the curriculum. Each interaction with our students is an opportunity to provide guidance that will help them function at a higher intellectual level. As a result of scaffolded assistance, our students internalize knowledge of content, strategies, and thinking dispositions, and how to put them to use productively. They take our voices with them to guide intelligent behavior in future tasks—and they become more intelligent.

REFERENCES

Argyris, C. (1993). *Knowledge for action: A guide to overcoming barriers to organizational change.* San Francisco: Jossey-Bass.

Beed, P.L., Hawkins, E.M., & Roller, C.M. (1991). Moving learners toward independence: The power of scaffolded instruction. *The Reading Teacher, 44,* 648-655.

Brown, J.S., Collins, A., & Duguid, P. (1989). Situated cognition and the culture of learning. *Educational Researcher, 18,* 32-42.

Collier, J.L., & Collier, C. (1974). *My brother Sam is dead.* New York: Scholastic.

Duffy, G.G., Roehler, L.R., & Herrmann, B.A. (1988). Modeling mental processes helps poor readers become strategic readers. *The Reading Teacher, 41,* 762-767.

Forbes, E. (1971). *Johnny Tremain.* New York: Dell.

Gardner, H. (1983). *Frames of mind: Conceptions of the nature of intelligence.* New York: Basic Books.

Gaskins, I.W., Anderson, R.C., Pressley, M., Cunicelli, E.A., & Satlow, E. (1993). The moves and cycles of cognitive process instruction. *Elementary School Journal, 93,* 277-304.

Gaskins, I.W., & Elliot, T.T. (1991). *Implementing cognitive strategy instruction across the school: The Benchmark manual for teachers.* Cambridge, MA: Brookline Books.

Goleman, D. (1995). *Emotional intelligence.* New York: Bantam Books.

Pearson, P.D., & Fielding, L. (1991). Comprehension instruction. In R. Barr, J.L. Kamil, P. Mosenthal, & P.D. Pearson (Eds.), *Handbook of reading research,* Vol. 11 (pp. 815-860). New York: Longman.

Perkins, D. (1995). *Outsmarting IQ: The emerging science of learnable intelligence.* New York: The Free Press.

Pinchot, G., & Pinchot, E. (1993). *The end of bureaucracy and the rise of the intelligent organization.* San Francisco: Berrett-Koehler.

Polya, G. (1957). *How to solve it* (2nd ed.). New York: Doubleday.

Pressley, M., El-Dinary, P.B., Gaskins, I.W., Schuder, T., Bergman, J.L., Almasi, J., & Brown, R. (1992). Direct explanation done well: Transactional instruction of reading comprehension strategies. *Elementary School Journal, 92,* 277-304.

Rogoff, B. (1990). *Apprenticeship in thinking: Cognitive development in social context.* New York: Oxford University Press.

Seligman, M.E.P. (1990). *Learned optimism.* New York: Simon & Schuster.

Senge, P.M. (1990). *The fifth discipline: The art and practice of the learning organization*. New York: Doubleday.

Sternberg, R.J. (1990). *Metaphors of mind: Conceptions of the nature of intelligence*. New York: Cambridge University Press.

Tharp, R.G., & Gallimore, R. (1988). *Rousing minds to life: Teaching, learning, and schooling in social context*. New York: Cambridge University Press.

Vygotsky, L.S. (1978). *Mind in society: The development of higher psychological processes* (J. Cole, V. John-Steiner, S. Scribner, & E. Souberman, Eds. & Trans.). Cambridge, MA: Harvard University Press.

Waitley, D. (1995). *Empires of the mind: Lessons to lead and succeed in a knowledge-based world*. New York: William Morrow.

Wick, C.W., & Leon, L.S. (1993). *The learning edge*. New York: McGraw-Hill.

Wood, D.J., Bruner, J.S., & Ross, G. (1976). The role of tutoring in problem solving. *Journal of Child Psychology and Psychiatry, 17* (2), 89-100.

CHAPTER THREE

Scaffolding Scientific Competencies within Classroom Communities of Inquiry

KATHLEEN HOGAN & MICHAEL PRESSLEY,
The University at Albany, State University of New York

Verbal transactions within classrooms are so routine and commonplace that it is easy to overlook their potential to transform a culture of learning. Yet teacher-to-student and student-to-student dialogues provide unparalleled opportunities for helping children learn how to think flexibly, critically, and reflectively. Particularly in inquiry-oriented, materials-centered science classrooms where text-based learning is deemphasized, dialogue is a key resource for fostering students' cognitive growth.

An alternative to the traditional recitation format (in which teachers ask students questions, the students respond, and the teacher evaluates the answer) is one in which the teacher becomes the students' conversational partner. The teacher enters into discussions with students in order to understand their thinking and move it along, rather than to evaluate it. The teacher provides verbal scaffolds—supports that enable students to build powerful thinking strategies and conceptual understanding. With prompting and supports, stu-

Thank you to Craig Altobell, Ric Campbell, and Jane Cappiello, whose masterful scaffolding of their students' science learning inspired these thoughts and provided excerpts of classroom dialogue.

dents become facile at thinking aloud to construct and clarify ideas. They become aware of *how*, not just *what*, they are thinking as the teacher highlights and labels their processes.

In an ongoing study of discourse in inquiry-based middle school science classrooms (Hogan, Pressley, & Nastasi, 1996), we are exploring the potential of thoughtful dialogue to promote student learning. Applications of constructivist learning theory to science education have emphasized hands-on experiences, with less focus on how verbal interactions can facilitate the construction of ideas. By examining the nature of dialogue in peer groups and between teachers and students in inquiry-based settings, we hope to gain an understanding of the links between talking and thinking about science that will lead to recommendations for classroom practice.

This chapter provides an overview of instructional scaffolding, suggests ways to expand scaffolding from one-to-one dialogues to whole-class settings, and offers some practical advice for teachers interested in building scaffolding into their pedagogical repertoires. Throughout the chapter, we share what we are learning from observing the practice of teachers who are committed to collaborating with their students in a process of scientific sense-making.

AN INTRODUCTION TO INSTRUCTIONAL SCAFFOLDING

A Few Moments in a Science Classroom

Picture this scenario: A sixth-grade science class is divided into seven groups of four students each to work on an investigation. Students are designing experiments to test what kind of leaves earthworms prefer to eat. They have a variety of materials at their desks, including maple and oak leaves, soil, cups, rulers, and scissors—materials that provide a structure and some hints to guide their deliberations about possible research designs.

The teacher circulates around the room, stops beside one group of students, listens to their discussion for a few seconds, and then decides to ask them a question. One of the students in the group responds to the teacher, one listens in, and the others continue to sort busily through the pile of leaves on their desks. The conversation goes like this:

TEACHER: Do you have a basic idea of how you'll design your experiment?

ALEX: Yes. We'll have two cups with the same amounts of dirt in them. One will have worms. One won't. We'll put three maple leaves in each.

TEACHER: But what if the leaves are not exactly the same? Maybe they came from different trees, or fell at different times. How could you make it really fair? Think about that.

ALEX: *(pause)* How about cutting them in half?

TEACHER: Well, nature's not perfect—one side might not be the same as the other. How could you be even more exact?

ALEX: *(pause)* Cut the leaf in little parts so one side's not bigger than the other?

TEACHER: Okay. Keep thinking about it. You guys are off to a good start.

This conversation has lasted less than two minutes. Meanwhile, other students' hands are up and pleas for teacher assistance are being sounded from four of the other groups. The teacher moves on, this time to respond to a question rather than to initiate one.

There is much to analyze in this brief event. What were the teacher's goals, strategies, and knowledge? Did any learning occur during the interchange? If so, what kind of learning happened and for whom? How did the learning occur? Did any of the group members learn by listening? By thinking aloud? How will the learning continue? Will everyone in the group eventually benefit from the conversation between Alex and his teacher?

This episode of instructional scaffolding focused on assisting the development of students' experimental design skills. We will look at this exchange more closely later, but even a preliminary analysis reveals that it is rich and complex, requiring a teacher's full awareness, insight, knowledge, abilities, and sensitivity. In short, the process of scaffolding demands the full range of good teaching skills (Pressley,

Hogan, Wharton-McDonald, Mistretta, & Ettenberger, 1996). Good scaffolding is also cognitively engaging for students, as it initiates and sustains a constructive and reflective process.

Similar scenarios occur numerous times throughout the school year in inquiry-based science classrooms. Yet a well-rounded science classroom includes many other instructional settings as well, including whole-class discussions, direct explanations, reading, and writing. Each of these provides different opportunities for teachers to foster the cognitive growth of their students, and each requires a context-sensitive scaffolding technique. Therefore, to be maximally useful, instructional scaffolding can be applied to the many settings, goals, constraints, and contextual realities teachers face.

Exploring the Scaffolding Metaphor

The assumption underlying instructional scaffolding is that there is a cognitive distance between what learners know and can do on their own, and what they are currently capable of doing with the assistance of a more knowledgeable person. The Soviet psychologist Vygotsky (1978; 1986) called this area of potential growth the learner's *zone of proximal development* (ZPD).

Scaffolding has come to be synonymous with a process of adult-child interaction within the child's ZPD (Stone, 1993). Early research on scaffolding was done in the context of parent/child interactions, which remains a strong focus for contemporary scaffolding research (e.g., Diaz, Neal, & Vachio, 1991; Pratt, Green, MacVicar, & Bountrogianni, 1992). These studies often concern preschoolers learning the goals and structure of novel tasks, not academic content (Hall, 1991). Another traditional focus for scaffolding research has been tutoring (Lepper, Aspinwall, Mummer, & Chabay, 1990; McArthur, Stasz, & Zmuidzinas, 1990; Wood, Bruner, & Ross, 1976). Rich descriptions of scaffolding by sensitive, responsive adults in one-to-one interactions with children have emerged from these bodies of research. (See Chapters 4 and 5 of this volume.)

The interaction between teacher and child in the child's ZPD serves the same role that physical scaffolding serves for a builder (Wood et al., 1976):

(1) it helps ensure the child's success,
(2) it extends the child's competence into new territory, and
(3) it can be taken away as the child becomes more responsible.

The metaphor of scaffolding translates to a model of learning through incremental assistance, with the prototypical interaction being one-to-one tutoring. The interactions create new meanings outside the heads of the two interacting people through the creation of a shared meaning, or *intersubjectivity* (Newman, Griffin, & Cole, 1989; Rogoff, 1990). These external meanings and interpersonal processes then become reconstructed internally, or *appropriated* (Rogoff, 1990). But scaffolding has to be seen as a complex collaborative process, in contrast to the traditional view of a teacher sequencing small steps for a child's ultimate attainment of new knowledge and skills. Ideally, scaffolding involves equal contributions by the adult and the child, resulting in a fluid communication process in which the emotional quality of the interpersonal relations and the values attached to the learning situation play important roles (Stone, 1993). The teacher or parent transmits cultural knowledge through scaffolding, but the receiver of the transmission is not passive. The child constructs personal knowledge through a dynamic teaching/learning interplay that draws the child into a more mature, yet still understandable, model of a problem (Rogoff, 1990). A key feature of the interaction is that the scaffolder provides just enough support for the learner to make progress on his or her own.

The conception that knowledge is constructed by learners during scaffolding extends Vygotskian concepts into the realm of Piagetian theory (Hatano, 1993). Science educators whose practice is informed by constructivism will find familiar ground here. The learners' search for meaning and significance are critical parts of their ZPDs (Moll & Whitmore, 1993). Yet to acknowledge that knowledge is individually constructed is not to ignore that this process is facilitated by interactions with other people—both horizontal relationships with equal-ability peers, and vertical interactions between expert and novice (Hatano, 1993). This blend of Vygotskian and Piagetian theories is known as *social constructivism* (Cobb, 1994; Driver, Asoko, Leach, Mortimer, & Scott, 1994). This perspective views scaffolding inter-changes as constructive all along the way, with meanings continually being created inside the heads of the speakers, rather than being created between them and then internalized. According to social constructivism, cognitive conflict and equilibration are central mecha-nisms of cognitive growth.

Yet another way to view scaffolding is provided by a *weaving* metaphor, which expands the idea of scaffolding beyond dyadic interaction into the community setting of the classroom, where multiple ZPDs are operating simultaneously (Brown, 1994). Con-sider a science teacher whose main goal is to induct novice students into a culture with very specific standards for making and evaluating knowledge claims. This teacher's classroom revolves around dialogic interchange that mirrors the practice of theory- and explanation-building in professional science. Yet the world of pre-college class-rooms is different from a professional scientific community (Reif & Larkin, 1991). Whereas professional scientists can keep the threads of an interchange of ideas together and connected to their own experi-ences and mental models, in a classroom the teacher must become both the loom and the master weaver to support students' integration of ideas. This approach to scaffolding will be discussed in detail later in this chapter.

THE INTRICACIES OF INSTRUCTIONAL SCAFFOLDING

Before exploring how scaffolding can be extended to support a community of learning, let's examine the basic components of instructional scaffolding more closely. The first column of Table 3-1 (on the next page) presents the dialogue between Alex and his teacher that was introduced in the beginning of this chapter. The second column describes the type and function of the language used by each of the participants.

The verbs describing the speech acts of the teacher (*asks, implies, hints, suggests, encourages*) indicate subtle cues that prompt the learner's active reflection and construction of ideas (Lepper et al., 1990; McArthur et al., 1990). The teacher uses forms of speech that cause the listener to form inferences (Stone, 1993). The inferences cause a tension which motivates the learner to interpret and make sense of what the teacher is implying. In order for this tension to be produc-

---

Table 3-1.
Analysis of a brief scaffolding episode.

Dialogue	Analysis
TEACHER: Do you have a basic idea of how you'll design your experiment?	*Asks a question to focus and monitor students' thinking.*
ALEX: Yes. We'll have two cups with the same amounts of dirt in them. One will have worms. One won't. We'll put three maple leaves in each.	*Articulates a plan.*
TEACHER: But what if the leaves are not exactly the same? Maybe they came from different trees, or fell at different times. How could you make it really fair? Think about that.	*Implies that there is more to consider. Hints at a problem area to focus on (i.e., assuring equal conditions in treatment and control groups).*
ALEX: *(pause)* How about cutting them in half?	*Generates a new idea.*
TEACHER: Well, nature's not perfect —one side might not be the same as the other. How could you be even more exact?	*Focuses attention on what needs to be considered. Prompts additional thinking.*
ALEX: *(pause)* Cut the leaf in little parts so one side's not bigger than the other?	*Refines original idea.*
TEACHER: Okay. Keep thinking about it. You guys are off to a good start.	*Acknowledges the idea. Encourages independent thinking.*

tive, however, there needs to be sufficient common ground—shared meanings and goals—between the teacher and the student (Stone, 1993). The teacher's cues and prompts succeed in causing the student to think, and thus the students' verbalizations are described using the verbs *articulates*, *generates*, *refines*.

We assume that the verbalizations of both the teacher and the student are preceded by covert thinking processes. What might the teacher be thinking before asking his first question, and indeed before each follow-up question? Most likely a very rapid but complex set of associations are made between his goals for the lesson (e.g., for students to learn how to design a controlled experiment); his assessment of the current status of the students' plans (e.g., how close they are to meeting the standard of a controlled experiment); his background knowledge about experimentation, leaves, and earthworms; and his knowledge of the overall competencies, needs, styles, and ZPDs of the students in the group.

Because the optimal level of support is different for each student, teachers must be well acquainted both with their students' needs and with the content they are teaching. Students vary in the amount of prompting they need, and in how close or *proximal* the next skill or knowledge level is for them. When a student's ZPD is narrow, the teacher may need to give more frequent and detailed hints (Day & Cordon, 1993). Students also differ in their ability to articulate what they are thinking and where they are having problems, making it more or less difficult for the teacher to respond appropriately. For example, there are cultural differences in the ways children interact during such exchanges (Kleifgen, 1988). In our example, since Alex is a willing and articulate conversational partner, his teacher can more easily diagnose his needs and pull his thinking along to a new stage.

What was going on for Alex during the interchange? In addition to constructing ideas by searching his prior knowledge and making new associations, Alex may have enjoyed basking in the teacher's attention. The teacher's presence and respectful engagement with the student's ideas undoubtedly bestowed some importance on the thinking that resulted, enriching the knowledge product with a positive emotional association. Indeed, our interviews with students reveal that they are better able to remember points when they associate them with the people and the context in which they emerged, and that they are more engaged and mindful in conversations with the teacher than with their peers.

The core elements of scaffolding, then, are sensitive provision of help only when needed, so that students do the parts of the task that they can accomplish alone, and the gradual ceding of problem-solving control from the teacher to the student (Day & Cordon, 1993). Characteristics of scaffolding that are critical to its success are *student ownership of the goals*, the *appropriateness* of the task for the student, *supportive instruction, shared responsibility* for the learning, and *internalization* of the products of the interchange (Langer, 1991). The essential elements of scaffolding can be summarized as follows (adapted from Applebee & Langer, 1983; Burns-Hoffman, 1993; Langer, 1991; Tharp & Gallimore, 1988; Wong, 1994; Wood et al., 1976).

- *Pre-engagement.* The teacher selects an appropriate task by anticipating student difficulties, needs, and strategies, and by considering curriculum goals.
- *Establishing a shared goal.* This motivational factor is crucial to the success of scaffolding. It requires a delicate balance between following the lead of the students and setting a course for them. Within the context of school it is the teacher's responsibility to set instructional goals. However, if a child doesn't own the same goal, or doesn't even understand it, then scaffolding won't work. In school situations in which children are *not* often engaged in spontaneous goal formation, scaffolding can become coercive (Searles, 1984) and potentially counterproductive.
- *Actively diagnosing the understandings and needs of the learner.* This requires not only a sensitivity to the learner, but also a firm grasp of the content area so as to compare the student's status to external standards for growth.

- *Providing tailored assistance.* Assistance might be in the form of questioning, cueing, prompting, coaching, modeling ideal performance, telling (direct instruction), or discussing. Through these verbal acts, the teacher adjusts the scaffolding to the student's needs. Many subtle acts of speech (some of which will be described later in this chapter) come into play.

- *Maintaining pursuit of the goal.* The more complicated a task is, the more support a student needs in order to stay focused and persistent. Teachers can maintain joint attention on a goal by requesting clarifications, asking questions, and so forth. They can also offer praise and encouragement to help bolster students' motivation.

- *Giving feedback.* A key role of the scaffolder is to summarize the progress that has been made and point out behaviors that led to the successes, expecting that eventually students will learn to monitor their own progress. One type of feedback is pointing out the distinction between the child's performance and the ideal. Another important type of feedback is attributing success to effort in order to encourage academically supportive attributions. Explicitly restating the concept that has been learned is another helpful form of feedback.

- *Controlling for frustration and risk.* The teacher needs to create an atmosphere in which there is freedom to try out alternatives without penalty. This establishes a safe environment in which mistakes are appreciated as part of the learning process. Commentary about the nature of the problem-solving process, such as "This is really complicated—it's normal to feel a little frustrated while you're trying to understand it," also helps students deal with frustration as part of the process of complex learning.

- *Assisting internalization, independence, and generalization to other contexts.* Assisting internalization of the learning means helping students become less dependent on the teacher's extrinsic signals for what to do next. The teacher can accomplish this goal by making students aware of signals intrinsic to the problem that point to the need for certain strategies (Perkins, 1986). Also, as teachers withdraw their support, they should make students aware of the need to consciously transfer their skills and knowledge to new contexts, and they should give them opportunities to do so.

Taken alone, each component of a scaffolding sequence is a familiar instructional strategy—but using them in combination results in more than the sum of the parts. These are not necessarily procedures to follow in lockstep succession. They can function more as general guidelines or a metascript (Tharp & Gallimore, 1988) for dynamic, flexible scaffolding.

THE CHALLENGES OF SCAFFOLDING IN CLASSROOM SETTINGS

There has been relatively little research done on scaffolding academic tasks in whole-class settings. Given the differences between classrooms and one-to-one settings on dimensions such as the emergence of goals, the emotional climate, and the audienced nature of performance, it is important to explore how scaffolding applies to the daily context within which most teachers operate. The following sections discuss some of these challenges.

Large classes. The sheer number of students in a large class poses a problem, since a teacher can't possibly interact for sustained periods of time with each individual student. But a further problem is that large classes present multiple zones of proximal development (Brown, 1994). Instruction pitched at some students' zones will be behind or beyond other students' zones. Also, the students most in need of academic help are least likely to seek it (Newman & Goldin, 1990), so it takes more effort to reach the full range of competencies in the classroom.

One way to manage the numbers problem is to organize students to work in groups as often as possible. This allows the teacher to scaffold groups rather than individuals, thereby making it feasible for each group to receive the teacher's attention during a single class period. However, all students do not necessarily engage with the teacher during group scaffolding. Another approach is to provide groups with tools—such as cue cards, question cards, or question stems—to help them scaffold one another (King, 1990). A key solution is to foster as much self-regulated learning as possible. The more students can regulate themselves, the more time the teacher can devote to those in need. Although students may not have sufficient background, experience, insight, or patience to diagnosis their peers' needs and provide scaffolded assistance, they can learn to prompt one another's thinking. Some students can be effective tutors, especially when given training, and often learn even more than the students they are tutoring (Semb, Ellis, & Araujo, 1993). Another method for applying the one-to-one scaffolding model to classrooms is whole-class scaffolding, which is described in detail later in this chapter.

Diverse communication styles. One issue related to large, heterogeneous classes involves the multiple perspectives of a culturally and linguistically diverse student body. Norms for interpersonal interactions vary from culture to culture, so different students may respond differently to probes from the teacher during scaffolding.

Even within culturally homogeneous groups, providing hints that facilitate progress without overdirecting is a challenge. The interaction becomes an exploratory process wherein the teacher tries out various prompts before hitting upon one that causes the student to make the desired inference. When initial prompts fail, the teacher must think of new ways of reasoning with the child about the task at hand. Through all of this, the teacher has to maintain a positive, caring tone while offering hints and suggestions that might all too easily be construed as criticisms. The process requires a lot of patience, which can be emotionally exhausting.

Finally, most students have a hard time understanding and articulating their thinking processes (Astington & Olson, 1990;

Flavell, Miller, & Miller, 1993), so the metacognitive aspects of scaffolded conversations present very real communication challenges. Teachers need to either circumvent abstract language such as "inferring" and "interpreting" and refer to thinking processes in more concrete terms (Pressley et al., 1992), or else make an effort to teach the meanings of their labels for cognitive processing.

Curriculum and time constraints. The scaffolding model advocates deep learning of complex content, which takes time. However, particularly at the secondary level, teachers are expected to cover an enormous amount of content—which often pushes teachers to move on to new topics before students have mastered the current topic. There are no ready solutions for this problem for individual teachers at the classroom level. Solving this problem will take nothing less than the combined efforts of teachers, administrators, parents, school boards, and state departments of education to move towards balancing depth with breadth of coverage.

Ownership of goals and uncertain endpoints. Some educators feel that scaffolding works best when the child initiates the interaction and stays in control of the language, with the adult acting in response (Searles, 1984). However, this type of scaffolding results in less teacher control over where the learning leads.

Although a teacher should hold goals for students' growth, it is essential to foster student ownership of the goals. It is equally important to support student-initiated goals. Uncertain endpoints can be made less uncertain by the teacher's masterful blending of a strong, guiding goal with sensitivity to learners' interests.

Student assessment. How can a teacher determine if the extra time and effort required by scaffolding is worth it, and then convince others that it is worthwhile? To help teachers justify their use of scaffolding, assessment needs to be more sensitive to the kinds of gains expected through scaffolding.

Since scaffolding hones students' thinking abilities, assessment of thinking *processes*, not just of products, should be done in order to document and provide feedback on the effects of scaffolding. Also, models of dynamic assessment (Day & Cordon, 1993) can be explored as fruitful ways to assess teaching for mastery through scaffolding.

Demands on teachers. Effective scaffolding requires extensive insights into individual learners, as well as solid pedagogical content knowledge (Shulman, 1986). Ideally, competent scaffolders understand the way experts solve problems within the discipline and have these competencies themselves. In order to scaffold effectively, teachers need to know what a child already knows, what competencies are within his or her reach, and what his or her misconceptions are. This is a demanding level of insight for just one student, let alone for a whole classroom of children. Teachers also need to know the curriculum well, have insights into where students are likely to have trouble, and understand the source of the trouble by probing behind students' incorrect answers. It can take years of experience to build up knowledge of all of the ways in which students can go wrong, which interventions help, and for whom.

In order to help build a corps of teachers who possess scaffolding skills, modeling of and instruction in scaffolding techniques should be strong parts of pre-service teacher education. In-service professional development and peer coaching can help build the scaffolding skills of experienced teachers. Freeing up more time in the day for teachers to plan and replenish their energy for interacting with students would go a long way towards encouraging and enabling the use of effortful instructional strategies such as scaffolding.

In summary, scaffolding is very demanding in ideal situations such as tutoring, and those demands are magnified when the ratio is one to twenty or thirty. In addition to being facile in the disciplinary area they are teaching, teachers must be expert pedagogues and communicators. Sustained across an entire school day, this approach takes a lot of energy and commitment.

WEAVING A CLASSROOM COMMUNITY OF INQUIRY

Thinking Together with Students

We've mentioned that opportunities for classroom teachers to work one-to-one with students for sustained periods of time are rare. Also, individual scaffolding is costly in terms of teacher time and effort, and it involves a trade-off between the *number* of students receiving the teacher's attention and the *intensity* of that attention. When a teacher does engage with individuals or small groups of students in an inquiry-based science setting, the interaction is usually brief due to competing demands for his or her attention (e.g., coordinating activities, watching the time, monitoring safety, managing materials, responding to questions, managing discipline, etc.). There often is not time for the teacher to listen to small-group discussions, provide hints, sensitively respond to the students' ideas, and then gradually fade assistance. The prototypical scaffolding model is impractical for day-to-day science instruction.

An alternative approach to scaffolding that better fits classroom realities shifts the focus from one-to-one interactions to interactions among the whole community of learners. This can be accomplished by scaffolding students' induction into the protocols of a community of inquiry. In this model, the whole social fabric of the classroom becomes the scaffolding that values, supports, and fosters the development of students' scientific competencies over time.

This whole-class perspective reflects a tradition of Soviet psychology which holds that an individual's thinking is profoundly influenced by participating in forms of social practice (Leonte'ev, 1981; Vygotsky, 1978). Viewing scaffolding as participation in a community of scientific discourse is quite different from viewing it as a form of cognitive strategies instruction (a view described in other chapters in this volume). The teacher's role within a community of inquiry is not so much to execute a set of specific strategies, but rather to organize the learning environment to establish an underlying culture that centers around thinking together with students.

The Language of Responsive Teaching

As in all scaffolding, whole-class scaffolding requires the mindful use of language with students. Teachers can make students' comments more meaningful by reacting to and elaborating on them. Such conversational partnerships allow students to build on and use the teacher's thinking process, so that they are able to think in more flexible and mature ways than they could do alone. Table 3-2 on the next page presents a list of the types of statements we have found that teachers use to facilitate student thinking during whole-class discussions.

When orchestrated according to the principles of instructional scaffolding, whole-class discussions can support and extend students' understanding and prompt them to think more deeply and in more complex ways. Whereas traditional whole-class discussions resemble a game of inferring what the teacher has in mind, scaffolded whole-class discussions allow students an opportunity to articulate their own understandings (Cobb, Wood, & Yackel, 1993). The teacher prods students to articulate what is behind their reasoning, prompting a constructive process. Meanwhile, as one student thinks aloud, his or her thoughts and exchanges with the teacher are witnessed by the rest of the class members, who are learning the scientific communal practices and social norms being modeled during the interchange.

As students practice and internalize the style of conversations they have with the teacher and other students in the thinking community, they start to talk to themselves in similar ways (Tharp & Gallimore, 1988). The products of the interchanges for individual students are not just new insights about the subject matter, but ways of thinking strategically, reflectively, and dialogically (Wertsch, 1991). The teacher's questions, such as "What are the connections between what you observed and what you already know?", become self-guided questions. The following words of psychologist Jerome Bruner (1966) illustrate this idea:

> It is not so much that a teacher provides a model to *imitate*. Rather, it is that the teacher can become part of the student's internal

Table 3-2.
Types of teacher statements that prompt student thinking.

- **Frames a problem or articulates a goal** ("It sounds to me that what you're trying to do is figure out why the force indicator had a higher reading the second time.")

- **Encourages attention to conflicts and differences of opinion** ("Jenny, Tom thinks the answer is *humid*, and you think it's *arid*. I want you to keep talking to each other to figure it out.")

- **Refocuses the discussion** ("So far we've agreed on one thing—let's consider data from the second experiment.")

- **Invites interaction of ideas** ("What's James asking? Who can expand on that?")

- **Prompts refinement of language** ("When you say *it* went up, what exactly are you referring to? What do you mean when you say *air pressure?*")

- **Turns question back to its owner** ("I don't know, what do you think?")

- **Communicates standards for explanations** ("I need to hear the evidence that backs up your claim.")

- **Asks for elaboration** ("So talk to us about the angles you mentioned.")

- **Asks for clarification** ("You need to tell me what you mean when you say *whatever the liquid consists of.*")

- **Restates or summarizes student statements** ("So you're saying that with a larger surface area and the same weight, the disk would move farther?")

dialogue—somebody whose respect he wants, whose standards he wishes to make his own. It is like becoming a speaker of a language one shares with somebody. The language of that interaction becomes a part of oneself, and the standards of style and clarity that one adopts for that interaction become a part of one's own standards (p. 124).

In classrooms where teachers practice thoughtful, whole-class scaffolding, we regularly observe behaviors which indicate that students are in the process of internalizing standards for scientific discussions. For instance, students may stop themselves in mid-sentence to say to the teacher, "Do you want me to explain what I mean by that?"—or simply pause and, without any prompting from the teacher, go back to clarify their terms or elaborate on their statements.

Let's look at effective whole-class scaffolding in more detail. In the following example from an eighth-grade physical science class, the teacher plays a central role in the discussion. It is early in the school year, and she feels that she needs to model productive dialogues for students so that later they will be able to guide their own discussions, in both whole-class and small-group settings. The teacher works with each student's thinking, while weaving other students into the interchange of ideas. She is the master weaver, holding threads of important ideas and bringing them back to the surface when they're dropped. She has in mind a very general design for the weaving, which enables her to return to previous ideas in order to move the group's thinking along. The details of the design, however, are determined by students' input. The teacher's capacity to keep several strands of the dialogue in mind reduces this burden on students. Rather than getting overwhelmed by or simply ignoring a good deal of potentially fruitful input—as often happens in unfacilitated small-group peer discussions—students in the teacher-facilitated discussion are able to engage with the full richness of ideas presented by their peers.

The focus of the unit being taught in the dialogue below is building mental models of the particulate nature of matter. Activities are aimed at creating a knowledge product, a model, such as scientists seek to develop. The excerpts begin in the middle of a class discussion trying to summarize and explain the results of a series of experiments on solids, liquids, and gases. The students have just recounted the results of a lab during which they saw supercooled water in a test tube freeze as soon as it was stirred. The teacher summarizes the observations that students have shared:

> TEACHER: It froze. So what we can say here is that water in a liquid form turned to ice, or to water in a solid form. That's kind of a summary of what we were observing. Does anyone want to comment more about that?
>
> JAKE: I have a question. When water gets frozen, it expands. What happens if you compress frozen water, will it change into a liquid?

Jake's question initiates a 15-minute discussion, during which students react to and build upon his idea while the teacher provides scaffolding for their exchanges. For the first three and a half minutes of the discussion, students describe how ice cube trays compress water, and how a liquid that is contained on all sides could cause the container to explode when the liquid freezes and expands, as happens when a bottle of soda freezes. After several students recount personal experiences with unexpected disasters due to freezing and expansion of liquids, the teacher refocuses the discussion:

> TEACHER: Let's go back to Jake's question. He asked *(signals to Jake to help her restate his question)*, if you compress water, because liquid water expands and takes up more space as ice ...
>
> JAKE: ... if you compressed it, would it turn back into a liquid form.

Teacher brings attention back to a central question; invites student to restate the question; student restates it.

- -

> TEACHER: ... would it turn back into a liquid form. *(Mirrors the hand gestures Jake uses to show compression.)* Anyone have

Teacher echoes the student verbally and with gestures, then

any ideas about that? Laura?

LAURA: How long would it take if it was warmer ... *(continues her thought, but is inaudible)*.

TEACHER: If we heated the ice, it would go back to liquid, but the question is if we applied pressure, would pressure put it back? What do you think, Isaac?

ISAAC: I think it would.

TEACHER: You think it would, if you applied enough pressure ...

ISAAC: ... not just on two sides, like on all four sides.

TEACHER: So you think that if we could apply enough pressure ... *(she is interrupted as a few students start to speak up)*. Now, let me hear what these two people have to say, and then I want to ask you another question. *(Nods to Michael, who has his hand up.)*

invites other students' input; student offers a response unrelated to the conditions specified in the original question; teacher confirms her statement, but brings focus back to the central question and invites additional input; student responds; teacher restates his response; he expands his thought; teacher restates expanded thought, then calls for additional input.

MICHAEL: Is it possible to have pure ice, without air in it, because doesn't an ice cube expand because they're taking the oxygen that was in the water, or no, the air that was in the water and then that causes it to expand?

TEACHER: So you think maybe the reason it expands is because of the air that might be contained in the ice cube.

MICHAEL: Is it possible to get an actual, a pure piece of ice that contains no oxygen, and so it, if that was right then ice wouldn't expand then, I mean I don't think it's right, but ...

Student brings up a new idea related to why water expands when it freezes; teacher restates his central idea; he expands his thinking.

TEACHER: See, what you're doing is suggesting that an experiment we might try is if we could get water that didn't have any gas in it and freeze that, and do you predict that it will still expand when it freezes, or do you predict that it will not, do you have any idea of what might happen?

MICHAEL: It probably still would expand then because I have a feeling that something else like air and water, like the molecules get bigger ...

Teacher labels his input according to protocols of scientific practice of testing hypotheses, and asks for a prediction; student offers a prediction along with additional thoughts.

TEACHER: Danny, you wanted to say something?

DANNY: Yeah, he was saying that getting ice without the oxygen, but ice is water and water has oxygen in it. *(Eruption of a lot of voices in reaction to this point, including Michael's own reaction.)*

JAKE: He said air.

DANNY: No, he said oxygen.

STUDENTS: Yeah.

TEACHER: So, ah, are you saying, maybe you better clarify this, we've been writing water as H_2O, Michael—when you're talking about air, oxygen and water, you're talking about this? *(She writes H_2O on the overhead.)*

MICHAEL: Yeah. So it would just be H. It would be H_2.

TEACHER: And Danny, you're saying that oxygen is always going to be there.

DANNY: Yeah.

MICHAEL: *(to Danny)* Why can't you just subtract that?

Teacher brings another student into the discussion; student points out a flaw in Michael's thinking; many students react; another student comments on what he heard Michael say; others disagree; teacher calls for a clarification; Michael responds and elaborates; teacher restates Danny's argument, calling for his confirmation that she has restated his point correctly; Michael and Danny talk directly to each

DANNY: It wouldn't be water, it wouldn't be ice. *(Other voices chime in to agree.)*	*other; Michael concedes Danny's point.*
MICHAEL: Oh yeah.	

TEACHER: One thing I want you to get, to become very accustomed to in this class, is what we want you to do is throw out ideas. Sometimes we may rip them apart, sometimes we may just go on to someone else, sometimes we might do lots of things.	*Teacher makes metacommentary on the purpose and practice of this type of interchange, which in part communicates the nature of scientific thinking, and in part serves to support student risk-taking and reduces the potential embarrassment for students who think aloud.*

The discussion continues, with new directions initiated by student questions, but also with students and the teacher making references back to Jake's original question about whether or not compressed ice would turn back to liquid water, and to Michael's question about the possibility of oxygen-free water.

Some additional types of statements made by the teacher as she facilitated the discussion are:

- *Clarifies assumptions behind statements to prompt students to examine them.* "Now if we were to take ice and compress it and get it to melt, does that mean we're removing the oxygen from the water?"
- *Summarizes a student's statement to invite confirmation that she understands the intent of the statement.* "So it's not the pushing together that's causing it to melt ..."
- *Relates a new statement to another student's previous statement.* EXAMPLE 1: "If you didn't have any air, which is kind of what Michael was asking, which was if you could get the air out.

But he was asking it in a little bit different direction. So you're saying if you have a container with just water, absolutely nothing else but water in there, and you freeze that, will it expand?"

EXAMPLE 2: "So Emma is disagreeing with you on two pieces [of ice], but she agreed with you with shattered pieces."

- *Highlights how questions can lead to investigations.* "That one we could actually try. We could try that and find out. That's a good question."

- *Metacommentary—makes the purpose of the style of dialogue explicit.*

  EXAMPLE 1. "You've proposed a lot of things that you've asked for answers to, and you're going to be really annoyed when you leave this class because you're not going to hear me giving many answers. However, everything we've been discussing is very, very important towards this model, so this discussion has not ended, and we can find out the answer to your questions, there are a couple of activities we could try to do, so let's come back to that at some point when it would fit into this."

  EXAMPLE 2. "I'm going to move on, I know that that's a source of frustration for you, but that's okay because it's going to be going all year like this. It doesn't mean that we aren't going to address your questions, because we are, in fact your questions are fairly fundamental questions to our understanding of this particular model that you're going to be developing and that you should explain to us so it makes sense."

A distinctive feature of this discussion is that the teacher does not *judge* the students' thinking, but rather engages with it to expand the surface area of ideas, and eventually to move students toward deeper understandings. While scaffolding the discussion, the teacher is supporting students' own thinking rather than compensating or substituting for a lack of thinking (Pressley et al., 1996). The teacher provides enough facilitation for students to make progress on their own. The dialogue is exploratory, supporting students in creating and discovering thoughts as they talk. They are not expected to express perfectly formed ideas.

Some of the mechanisms that govern how and why learning occurs during thoughtful dialogues are revealed through an analysis of what students are doing as they participate. Students are:

- articulating and clarifying ideas,
- relating new ideas to prior knowledge,
- connecting their own thoughts to others' ideas,
- elaborating on ideas, and
- providing explanations.

Although academic discourse can be cognitively demanding for students, it can also stimulate their cognitive growth.

We can summarize some of the salient characteristics of scaffolded whole-class discussions in a community of inquiry as follows (Langer, 1991):

1. Students are treated as thinkers who have something to offer.
2. Question generating, not just producing right answers, is a central aim.
3. Students' understanding, not just their memory of facts, is tapped.
4. The teacher's response is dedicated to furthering understanding, not to evaluating and reviewing.
5. There is a move towards independence of student thinking, with support given only when necessary in order to encourage students' ability to initiate their own thoughtful participation in a community exchange of ideas.

In successful academic discussions, teachers maintain a balance between a student-centered and a subject-centered focus, for instance by upholding the standards of scientific discourse while enabling each child's participation.

It is evident that such discussions can foster competencies that are valued by science educators. Certainly students are dealing with important ideas, as in the above discussion, which was intended to move students toward an understanding of matter and molecules. The national standards also call for development of students' science process skills, as well as more general thinking skills, or habits of mind (American Association for the Advancement of Science, 1993; National Research Council, 1996). During the above discussion, students were reflecting on their laboratory observations, thinking about how to test new ideas, and developing habits of critical judgment. Science education standards also present a goal for students to generalize from their own experiences in order to understand the role of inquiry in scientific work, and to gain a range of historical and contemporary perspectives on the nature of scientific knowledge and practices. The teacher's metacommentary helps in this regard, making the purpose of the dialogue explicit and pointing out similarities to the ways scientists construct knowledge. In this way, students' learning about the nature of science is grounded in their own experiences.

Finally, the national standards emphasize encouraging student motivation and volition to learn science. Evidence that these discussions are motivating comes from indicators of student engagement during discussions such as the one recounted above. Our analyses of videotapes show nonverbal signs of student engagement; students make comments such as "Awww ... it was just getting good" when the class ends; and in interviews students can describe the characteristics of discussions that keep them mentally engaged. This is not to claim that scaffolded whole-class discussions are engaging at all times for all students. However, dynamic whole-class discussions can promote active listening, if not necessarily verbal participation, from the majority of the class.

The Flexibility of the Community Scaffolding Approach

Scaffolded whole-class discussions can accommodate a range of teaching philosophies and goals. In our study of discourse patterns in science classrooms, we've seen that thoughtful dialogue can be accomplished in a variety of ways. For instance, the teacher who facilitated the discussion recounted above adheres to the tenets of radical constructivism (von Glasersfeld, 1993). Throughout her mental model building unit on matter, she does not indicate to students when their notions about atoms and molecules are right or wrong. She also does not introduce or explain concepts; she believes that in order for students to learn in a deep and meaningful way, they must refine their own abilities to judge ideas based on evidence, rather than relying on her scientific authority. She sets up experiments and demonstrations from which students induce principles. She actively monitors individual students, small groups, and the class as a whole, diagnosing how their thinking needs to be expanded. Her style of promoting student thinking is captured accurately by one of her students during an interview: "She doesn't teach us, she just asks us questions."

Another teacher in our study who also engages in thoughtful dialogue with students uses a less radical style of constructivism. His exchanges with students are peppered with bits of information, summaries, and explanations of concepts. His scaffolding style is determined in part by his school's curriculum, testing, and evaluation constraints that require him to move students along as efficiently as possible while fostering understanding. A key feature of his ability to stimulate students' cognitive engagement is that his direct explanations follow his diagnoses of students' needs, rather than being offered in an authoritative or disconnected manner.

In addition to a continuum of how much conceptual information the teacher infuses into discussions, there is also a continuum of centrality of the teacher's role during scaffolded whole-class discussions. In the dialogue we cited, the teacher was at the center of the discussion like a telephone operator taking, transferring, and connecting calls. But teachers can also step out of a central role, while still upholding standards for the conversation and assisting from the sidelines when necessary.

In one such class session, the teacher had students bring their desks into a circle and asked them to share and discuss explanations of their lab results. He told them to direct their comments to each other, rather than to him. Occasionally he offered comments to facilitate their process, such as, "I'm going to interject for a second. You're all trying to talk over each other. Take the time to say your ideas clearly. I didn't hear Jason, but he tried to say something. Also, as a listener, I need you to define your terms." At another point, after an awkward silence, one student said to the teacher: "The conversation died." The teacher responded, "So what point have we come to? Why did it die? Are all the ideas on the table? I want you to keep talking. It seems to me that there is still disagreement. I want you to agree on one best explanation." After the teacher made these comments, the students picked up and expanded their conversation.

The presence of the teacher was crucial to the maintenance of the students' focus, yet the students also had a great deal of responsibility for orchestrating their own discussion. This tactic can be a stepping stone for students between relying on the teacher at the center of a whole-class discussion, and having productive discussions without the teacher present at all, such as is often necessary during small-group work.

STUDENTS' PERSPECTIVES

What do students think about scaffolding? In order to discover students' perspectives on learning through dialogues with their peers and teacher, our study included interviews with students to complement our classroom observations. Here is one student's response to a question about what it is like when a teacher interacts with a small group that is engaged in problem solving:

> It's annoying because if we think we have it figured out then she asks
> another question and we get all confused, so it makes us confused, but
> it also, I guess, helps us 'cause then we can get a stronger model. Or
> if we have questions and she won't really answer them, that's
> annoying, too.

These complaints are slightly disingenuous, coming from an adolescent who would rather not let on that schoolwork can be exciting, or that she has a curious mind beneath her facade of adolescent ennui. Indeed, her portrayal of her teacher as a sort of gadfly (defined as one who "annoys or stirs up from lethargy") is quite accurate.

Most students feel that they have to meet different standards of explanation when talking to the teacher than when talking to peers, as is revealed in the following comment:

> The way you'd explain it to a teacher is different from the way you'd
> explain it to a friend. If the teacher asks how big the earth is, you'd
> have to be like "It's really big, compared to this," but if you were to
> talk to someone else you'd be like, "You know, it's just REALLY big."
> You don't have to explain it as much with your friends as you do with
> a teacher.

Many students tell us during interviews that when talking to the teacher they try their best to say something intelligent, whereas within their peer groups their thinking and talking is typically more lax. Although we see value in—and real gains from—students' struggles to form and articulate ideas together without teacher intervention, both our observations and our interviews highlight the crucial role of the teacher as upholder, communicator, and supporter of standards for scientific thinking.

We are finding that students' perspectives on the nature of knowledge and the purpose of social dialogue about ideas are critical components of the scaffolding equation. For instance, while the teacher may be operating from a constructivist philosophy, not all students share a similar belief that knowledge is constructed rather than transmitted. Being explicit about the purpose of the probes used during scaffolding, and about expectations for students' roles as thinkers, is extremely important. This type of explanation is emerging as a key element of an intervention we are beginning to design to improve students' ability to engage in dialogic learning.

HOW TO BEGIN

Instructional scaffolding is not a whole new approach to teaching so much as it is a framework that unifies the elements of responsive teaching. Scaffolding requires as much attention to creating a classroom context that supports thinking as to implementing specific instructional strategies. Since talking is externalized thinking, engaging in instructional dialogues with students is one of the most powerful tools teachers have to shape students' cognitive processes.

Becoming proficient at scaffolding takes time. Here are a few suggestions for how to begin to develop the necessary skills:

1. *Examine your beliefs about the teaching/learning process.* Does scaffolding fit with your professional beliefs and goals, the demands you face, and the goals of your school and community? The subsoil in which strong, flexible teaching grows is a teacher's own philosophy of education. Scaffolding will work best as part of an entire system of pedagogy rooted in a unifying philosophy. Scaffolding needs to be integrated into your belief system so that you develop a personal theory that is a creative synthesis of educational theories and your personal experience (Brammer & Shostrom, 1982; Hunt, 1987).

2. *Listen to your dialogues.* Who is doing the thinking during your class discussions? How often do your responses to students probe their thinking rather than close down their thinking? How many students do you have participating in these discussions? A general question to guide your self-

monitoring is: Am I talking at a level that enables each child to participate actively?

3. *Internalize a framework for scaffolding.* General scaffolding strategies such as setting goals, focusing attention, prompting responses, and so on can be used flexibly once they are internalized.

4. *Work on creating a pervasive atmosphere of thoughtfulness.* Create a classroom culture that celebrates thinking as exciting, and as the central purpose of schooling.

5. *Create a structure that works for scaffolding.* For instance, in addition to whole-class discussions, practice using scaffolding during peer-group tasks in smaller groups.

6. *Make your scaffolding strategies explicit to students.* A scaffolder need not be a puppeteer. Discuss with students why you talk with them the way you do so that they understand that the purpose is to cause them to think. This will also help them take responsibility for their end of the scaffolding partnership.

7. *Practice, reflect, and welcome your own mistakes as part of your learning process.*

POINTS TO EXPLORE THROUGH FUTURE RESEARCH AND REFLECTIVE PRACTICE

Given the relatively recent turn of researchers' attention to scaffolding in classroom settings, many questions remain to be explored. These include:

- What is the optimal blend of scaffolding with other instructional strategies such as discovery learning and direct explanation?
- Are the mechanisms that make scaffolding effective during tutoring similar to those at work in whole-class settings?
- Are some academic goals better facilitated by scaffolding than others?

- What are the affective and motivational underpinnings and outcomes of scaffolding?
- Is it possible for whole-class discussions to scaffold the thinking of the entire range of students within the classroom?

Current research, including our own and others' being done in natural classroom settings (e.g., Cobb et al., 1993; Gallas, 1995; O'Connor & Michaels, 1993), indicates that using scaffolding to create productive communities of learning is a vibrant future direction for educational research and practice.

REFERENCES

American Association for the Advancement of Science (1993). *Benchmarks for science literacy.* New York: Oxford University Press.

Applebee, A.N., & Langer, J.A. (1983). Instructional scaffolding: Reading and writing as natural language activities. *Language Arts, 60,* 168-175.

Astington, J.W., & Olson, D.R. (1990). Metacognitive and metalinguistic language: Learning to talk about thought. *Applied Psychology: An International Review, 39,* 77-87.

Brammer, L.M., & Shostrom, E.L. (1982). *Therapeutic psychology: Fundamentals of counseling and psychotherapy* (4th ed.). Englewood Cliffs, NJ: Prentice-Hall.

Brown, A.L. (1994). The advancement of learning. *Educational Researcher, 23,* 4-12.

Bruner, J.S. (1966). *Toward a theory of instruction.* Cambridge, MA: Harvard University Press.

Burns-Hoffman, R. (1993, March). *Scaffolding children's informal expository discourse skills.* Paper presented at the Biennial Meeting of the Society for Research in Child Development, New Orleans, LA.

Cobb, P. (1994). Where is the mind? Constructivist and sociocultural perspectives on mathematical development. *Educational Researcher, 23,* 13-20.

Cobb, P., Wood, T., & Yackel, E. (1993). Discourse, mathematical thinking, and classroom practice. In E.A. Forman, N. Minick, & C.A. Stone (Eds.), *Contexts for learning: Sociocultural dynamics in children's development* (pp. 91-119). New York: Oxford University Press.

Day, J.D., & Cordon, L.A. (1993). Static and dynamic measures of ability: An experimental comparison. *Journal of Educational Psychology, 85,* 75-82.

Diaz, R.M., Neal, C.J., & Vachio, A. (1991). Maternal teaching in the zone of proximal development: A comparison of low- and high-risk dyads. *Merrill-Palmer Quarterly, 37,* 83-108.

Driver, L., Asoko, H., Leach, J., Mortimer, E., & Scott, P. (1994). Constructing scientific knowledge in the classroom. *Educational Researcher, 23,* 5-12.

Flavell, J.H., Miller, P.H., & Miller, S.M. (1993). *Cognitive development* (3rd ed.). Englewood Cliffs, NJ: Prentice-Hall.

Gallas, K. (1995). *Talking their way into science: Hearing children's questions and theories, responding with curricula.* New York: Teachers College Press.

Hall, E.A. (1991, April). *An examination of the process of teaching reading to learning disabled children: Vygotskian perspectives.* Paper presented at the annual meeting of the American Educational Research Association, Chicago, IL.

Hatano, G. (1993). Time to merge Vygotskian and constructivist conceptions of knowledge acquisition. In E.A. Forman, N. Minick, & C.A. Stone (Eds.), *Contexts for learning: Sociocultural dynamics in children's development* (pp. 153-166). New York: Oxford University Press.

Hogan, K., Pressley, M., & Nastasi, B.K. (1996, April). *Discourse patterns and scaffolding strategies that support and inhibit student thinking during collaborative scientific inquiry.* Paper presented at the annual meeting of the American Educational Research Association, New York, NY.

Hunt, D. (1987). *Beginning with ourselves: In practice, theory, and human affairs.* Cambridge, MA: Brookline Books.

King, A. (1990). Enhancing peer interaction and learning in the classroom through reciprocal questioning. *American Educational Research Journal, 27,* 64-68.

Kleifgen, J.A. (1988). Learning from student teachers' cross-cultural communicative failures. *Anthropology and Education Quarterly, 19,* 218-234.

Langer, J.A. (1991). *Literacy understanding and literature instruction* (Report Series 2.11). Albany, NY: Center for the Learning and Teaching of Literature.

Leonte'ev, A.N. (1981). The problem of activity in psychology. In J.V. Wertsch (Ed.), *The concept of activity in Soviet psychology* (pp. 37-71). Armonk, NY: Sharpe.

Lepper, M.R., Aspinwall, L.G., Mummer, D.L., & Chabay, R.W. (1990). Self-perception and social-perception processes in tutoring: Subtle social control strategies of expert tutors. In J. M. Olson & M.P. Zann (Eds.), *Self-inference processes: The Ontario symposium* (pp. 217-237). Hillsdale, NJ: Erlbaum & Associates.

McArthur, D., Stasz, C., & Zmuidzinas, M. (1990). Tutoring techniques in algebra. *Cognition and Instruction, 7,* 197-244.

Moll, L.A., & Whitmore, K.F. (1993). Vygotsky in classroom practice: Moving from individual transmission to social transaction. In E.A. Forman, N. Minick, & C.A. Stone (Eds.), *Contexts for learning: Sociocultural dynamics in children's development* (pp. 19-42). New York: Oxford University Press.

National Research Council. (1996). *National science education standards.* Washington, DC: National Academy Press.

Newman, D., Griffin, P., & Cole, M. (1989). *The construction zone: Working for cognitive change in school.* New York: Cambridge University Press.

Newman, R.S., & Goldin, L. (1990). Children's reluctance to seek help with schoolwork. *Journal of Educational Psychology, 82,* 92-100.

O'Connor, M.C., & Michaels, S. (1993). Aligning academic task and participation status through revoicing: Analysis of a classroom discourse strategy. *Anthropology and Education Quarterly, 24,* 318-335.

Perkins, D. (1986). Thinking frames: An integrative perspective on teaching cognitive skills. In J.B. Baron & R.S. Sternberg (Eds.), *Teaching thinking skills: Theory and practice* (pp. 41-61). New York: W.H. Freeman.

Pratt, M.W., Green, D., MacVicar, J., & Bountrogianni, M. (1992). The mathematical parent: Parental scaffolding, parenting style, and learning outcomes in long-division mathematics homework. *Journal of Applied Developmental Psychology, 13,* 17-34.

Pressley, M., Hogan, K., Wharton-McDonald, R., Mistretta, J., & Ettenberger, S. (1996). The challenges of instructional scaffolding ... the challenges of instruction that supports student thinking. *Learning Disabilities Research and Practice, 11,* 138-146.

Pressley, M., El-Dinary, P.B., Gaskins, I., Schuder, T., Bergman, J.L., Almasi, J., & Brown, R. (1992). Beyond direct explanation: Transactional instruction of reading comprehension strategies. *Elementary School Journal, 92,* 511-554.

Reif, F., & Larkin, J.H. (1991). Cognition in scientific and everyday domains: Comparison and learning implications. *Journal of Research in Science Teaching, 28,* 733-760.

Rogoff, B. (1990). *Apprenticeship in thinking: Cognitive development in social context.* New York: Oxford University Press.

Searles, D. (1984). Who's building whose building? *Language Arts, 61,* 480-483.

Semb, G.B., Ellis, J.A., & Araujo, J. (1993). Long-term memory for knowledge learned in school. *Journal of Educational Psychology, 85,* 305-316.

Shulman, L. (1986). Paradigms and research programs in the study of teaching: A contemporary perspective. In M.C. Wittrock (Ed.), *Handbook of research on teaching* (3rd ed.; pp. 3-36). New York: Macmillan.

Stone, C.A. (1993). What is missing in the metaphor of scaffolding? In E.A. Forman, N. Minick, & C.A. Stone (Eds.), *Contexts for learning: Sociocultural dynamics in children's development* (pp. 169-183). New York: Oxford University Press.

Tharp, R.G., & Gallimore, R. (1988). *Rousing minds to life.* New York: Cambridge University Press.

von Glasersfeld, E. (1993). Questions and answers about radical constructivism. In K. Tobin (Ed.), *The practice of constructivism in science education* (pp. 23-38). Washington, DC: AAAS Press.

Vygotsky, L.S. (1978). *Mind in society.* Cambridge, MA: Harvard University Press.

Vygotsky, L.S. (1986). *Thought and language.* Cambridge, MA: MIT Press.

Wertsch, J.V. (1991). *Voices of the mind.* Cambridge, MA: Harvard University Press.

Wong, S. (1994). *Characterizing teacher-student interaction in Reading Recovery lessons* (Reading Research Report No. 17). Athens, GA: National Reading Research Center.

Wood, S.S., Bruner, J.S., & Ross, G. (1976). The role of tutoring in problem solving. *Journal of Child Psychology and Psychiatry, 17,* 89-100.

CHAPTER FOUR

Scaffolding Techniques of Expert Human Tutors

MARK R. LEPPER, MICHAEL F. DRAKE, &
TERESA O'DONNELL-JOHNSON, Stanford University

The art of teaching is the art of assisting discovery.
— MARK VAN DOREN

BACKGROUND

For most of recorded history, the primary method for the formal education of children was the individual tutorial. When Plato wrote about education among the ancient Greeks, his model was Socrates tutoring the slave boy; and when Philip of Macedonia conquered the Greeks, one of his first acts was to name Aristotle a tutor for his son Alexander. Many centuries later, when Rousseau sought to illustrate his views on educating the young, he did so by presenting hypothetical dialogues between the young child Émile and his personal tutor. At Oxford and Cambridge Universities, among many other distinguished institutions of learning around the world, work with indi-

Preparation of this chapter and the conduct of the research it reports were supported in part by Research Grant HD-25258 from the National Institute of Child Health and Human Development to the senior author. The authors wish to express their appreciation to Ralph Putnam for generously sharing with us the protocols in the course of his research, and to Maria Woolverton for her work in collecting many of the other protocols for our project. The ideas expressed here have benefited greatly from extensive discussions with Ruth Chabay, Jean-Luc Gurtner, Paul Whitmore, and Maria Woolverton. Thanks are also due to Paul Whitmore for his extensive comments on an earlier draft of this manuscript. Queries may be sent to Mark R. Lepper, Dept. of Psychology, Jordan Hall—Building 420, Stanford University, Stanford, CA 94305-2130.

vidual tutors comprises the bulk of post-secondary education.

To this day, individual tutoring is still commonly regarded as the "gold standard" of education—a procedure against which the value and effectiveness of other instructional methods can profitably be measured. As Benjamin Bloom (1984) has pointed out, individual tutoring has been shown to produce dramatic gains—changes of up to two full standard deviations on relevant measures of academic performance. These changes illustrate the magnitude of the improvements that can be obtained through instruction under essentially "optimal" conditions. Yet effects of this size are almost never reported in studies of other educational techniques. Hence, Bloom argues, the central challenge for our educational system is designing and developing instructional techniques that can be implemented on the large scale of compulsory education, but that will yield the same learning gains that individual tutoring sessions appear to produce.

Clearly, the remarkable instructional effectiveness of individual tutoring comes at a price. One-on-one relationships are expensive. In the past, tutoring proved a satisfactory educational alternative mainly because formal education was reserved for a small and elite segment of the population. Not surprisingly, shortly after the advent of the modern desire for compulsory universal education beginning in the mid-19th century, the search began for more cost-effective educational alternatives to apply to large groups of children. Personal tutoring was effectively reserved for very rich students, whose parents could afford to pay for such services, and very remedial students, whose scholastic deficiencies were sufficiently great to demand some special attention within the school.

As a result, at least in this country, remarkably little attention has been given to the study of individual tutorials. Although the beneficial outcomes of individual tutorials have been documented empirically, almost no studies, until recently, had tried to examine and identify the processes that underlie these benefits. In fact, when we began our own work on tutoring expertise, the most pertinent references we could locate were a set of elegant and thoughtful papers by Alan Collins and his associates (e.g., Collins & Stevens, 1982;

Stevens, Collins, & Goldin, 1982) examining *hypothetical* tutoring situations. In these studies, expert adult tutors had been asked to describe the techniques they would use to tutor a student on a particular subject. However, while these studies were quite revealing about many of the strategies and preferences of these tutors, they obviously provided little information about the critical processes by which tutors respond to errors and scaffold learning when students continue to have difficulties.

Prior to our own research, virtually no studies had examined the dynamic process of learning through individual tutorials. The only major exceptions to this assertion were the early studies on the ways mothers assisted their young children in performing novel and complex tasks—studies in which David Wood, Jerome Bruner, and their colleagues (Wood, Bruner, & Ross, 1976; Wood & Middleton, 1975; Wood, Wood, & Middleton, 1978) first introduced the metaphor of "scaffolding" learning. It is fitting that this metaphor should provide the unifying theme for this volume, because it has become so influential and pervasive in the educational literature (Berk & Winsler, 1995).[1]

For Wood et al. (1976), tutoring seemed to involve

> a kind of "scaffolding" process that enables a child or novice to solve a problem, carry out a task, or achieve a goal which would be beyond his unassisted efforts ... This scaffolding consists essentially of the

---

[1] The scaffolding metaphor can sometimes be confusing. For one thing, it is easy to construct misleading analogies. For example, if one imagines the temporary supporting platforms used by painters, builders, and window-washers to reach the higher floors of a building, one may conceptualize the tutor as providing supports upon which students can "reach higher" than they would otherwise be able. While such an image captures the enabling effects of instructional scaffolding, it also carries the inappropriate connotation that the learner (like the painter or the window-washer) will return to ground level when the scaffolding is removed.

Moreover, this term can be confusing even within the field of education research, because it appears to mean very different things to different authors (cf. Berk & Winsler, 1995). For some the term "scaffolding" applies to a domain of teacher actions nearly as broad as the term "tutoring" itself; for others, it has a much narrower application to particular techniques or strategies that tutors may use to support learning.

The most useful version of the metaphor that we have found refers to scaffolding as the sorts of temporary structures that are used to support arches or tunnels under construction, but which later, once construction is complete, can be removed without danger of the arch or tunnel subsequently collapsing. We thank Paul Whitmore for this suggestion.

adult "controlling" those elements of the task that are initially beyond the learner's capacity, thus permitting him to concentrate upon and complete only those elements that are within his range of competence.

(p. 90)

In this manner, they argued, not only could the child's immediate efforts be brought to a successful conclusion, but, in the long run, this sort of experience should permit the child to acquire new competencies more quickly and easily than other instructional techniques.

Given the evident effectiveness of individual tutoring, the lack of further information on the dynamics of the tutoring process seemed to us a striking omission in the literature on successful instructional methods. Such information should help us better understand the strategies and procedures by which successful tutors produce such exceptional results. Detailed studies of the procedures of highly effective tutors working with individual students, we thought, should enhance our understanding of the strategies and techniques these tutors use to produce such exceptional results. More generally, these studies should provide an illuminating laboratory for studying the dynamics of teaching strategies and learning processes.

GENERAL METHODOLOGY OF THE PRESENT STUDIES

As a consequence, over the past several years, a number of us at Stanford have conducted a detailed examination of the overall goals, the general strategies, and the specific motivational and instructional techniques of demonstrably expert and effective human tutors. In these research projects, we have watched and taped several dozen experienced tutors working with varying numbers of individual students, in tutoring sessions that lasted from 30 to 60 minutes each. We have been particularly interested in students who have had a history of academic difficulties in the subject being taught. Although many procedural details varied across the different studies, all projects shared the following general procedures and characteristics.

Tutors

For our research, we were especially interested in the actions and beliefs of experienced and truly expert tutors. To locate such subjects, we asked schools and tutoring agencies with good reputations in our community to suggest people who were considered really excellent teachers or tutors. We then asked these recommended tutors to engage in a series of individual tutoring sessions with a number of students, under laboratory conditions in which the tutors' and tutees' actions could be observed and videotaped. The tutors initially nominated varied considerably in their success. Those who proved most successful in working with a variety of tutees were designated as our most "expert" tutors. Our goals have been to characterize the goals, strategies, and techniques that these effective tutors employ, and to contrast their thoughts and actions with those of equally experienced, but less successful, tutors.

Subject Matter

The subject matter for all of our tutoring sessions involved elementary-level mathematics. We chose mathematics as the arena of study for two reasons: it is a highly organized domain, and it is the domain in which students' difficulties and misunderstandings have been most extensively studied. Across different samples, the particular topics have ranged from basic addition and subtraction, most appropriate for children in the early primary grades, to fairly complex multi-stage word-problems, more suited to children in the later primary grades.

Student Tutees

Because we were particularly interested in the strategies and techniques expert tutors use with the most challenging students, we primarily selected students identified by prior school performance and/or aptitude test scores in mathematics as requiring substantial remediation. (In our most recent studies, we have observed the same tutors working with samples of children selected to represent both the upper and the lower 20% of their classes in math, in order to permit clear comparisons between the two cases. At this writing, though, the results of these procedures have been subject only to very preliminary analysis.)

In addition to these general selection criteria, we attempted to ensure that all tutees fell in an appropriate "window for learning" in the specific area of mathematics under study. For this purpose, several weeks prior to the tutoring sessions, all potential students were administered a pre-test assessing their competence at the designated activity. Students were eligible for inclusion only if their pre-tests demonstrated that they (1) had mastered the prerequisite component skills that the material required, but also (2) had not yet fully mastered the material itself. For instance, students who were to be tutored in elementary addition with carrying needed to demonstrate a good knowledge of simple single-digit addition, but not yet be proficient in more complex problems involving carrying.

PROCEDURE

Tutoring sessions took place either at the children's own schools or in our tutoring laboratory at the Department of Psychology at Stanford. In both cases, the procedure was roughly the same. Prior to the sessions, tutors were informed about the subject matter to be addressed and, in most cases, were shown the student's pre-test. The student and the tutor were then seated along the same side of a rectangular work table, on which any written work was to be completed.

Two video cameras filmed the entire tutoring session. One camera was aimed from the ceiling directly toward the work surface of the table; the other was positioned to record the facial expressions and general bodily movements of the tutor and tutee. Outputs from these two cameras were then passed through an electronic screen-splitting device, permitting them to be recorded side by side on a single videotape. Subsequent analyses of the two channels could then be undertaken either separately or in conjunction.

After each session, once the student had left the room, the tutor was shown the complete videotape of the tutoring session he or she had just finished. During this viewing, the tutor was asked to provide a running verbal commentary on what the student might have been thinking and/or feeling as the session progressed, when the tutor had made an explicit choice in response to a particular event, and what goals had motivated their choices of tutoring procedures at various points in the session. These stimulated-recall "think-aloud" protocols were, in turn, tape-recorded for future analysis.

Measures

From the videotapes and transcripts of the tutoring sessions, as well as from the tests administered outside the tutoring sessions, a wide array of motivational and cognitive variables were assessed. We determined the success of individual tutoring sessions based on two major criteria for student improvement. To assess *cognitive* or informational gains, we relied primarily on changes in students' performance from before to after the tutoring sessions on standard written tests of the material under study. These tests were completed by each student outside the tutoring situation and in the tutor's absence. To measure *affective* or motivational gains, we relied primarily on ratings of the student's affect and motivational states at various points during the tutoring sessions, as assessed by "blind" observers (i.e., observers shown only the student's reactions, not the tutor's actions).

To analyze the actions and performance of tutors during these sessions, we performed a variety of complementary analyses, many of which will be discussed in more detail below. In general terms, these analyses focused on how tutors developed and selected problems to present, the particular ways in which they presented those problems, the manner in which they offered assistance and responded to student successes and errors, and the attempts they made to articulate and instruct students in the principles underlying problem solution. At each of these levels, we examined each tutor's actions and decisions from both a cognitive (informational) and an affective (motivational) perspective, using coding and rating systems that enabled different observers of the same protocol to arrive reliably at a common analysis.

Through a combination of these complementary analyses and measures, we sought to identify the primary goals, general strategies, and specific techniques employed by our most successful tutors. Before we examine the specific strategies and techniques, however, it will be useful to discuss some very general findings from our project. These findings fall into three categories. First, we show that it is indeed a reasonable goal to try to understand the dynamics of "expert" tutoring. Second, we describe the general structure of the tutoring sessions within which we have examined the goals and strategies of our expert tutors. Third, we demonstrate that the continuing interplay of cognitive and motivational considerations is critical in determining expert tutors' actions. These three sets of background findings form the basic foundation on which our subsequent, more detailed analyses are based.

IDENTIFICATION OF EXPERT TUTORS

The first general finding from our project is that "expert" tutors do seem to exist—that is, some tutors seem to be highly effective in working with a variety of different students, even when those students display a wide range of initial achievements and attitudes. Note that when we began our research, there was no guarantee that this would be the case. It could have turned out that different tutors were most effective with different types of students—that some tutors, for example, were particularly effective with remedial students and others were most effective with gifted tutees.

A second, related finding is that these "expert" tutors score highly on independent measures of instructional *and* motivational effectiveness. Their tutees, on average, not only learn more of the material; they also show increased interest and enthusiasm for the material. Again, although this outcome may not seem surprising, we should recall that it need not have been the case. For example, several of our less successful tutors seem highly effective in interesting and motivating students, but relatively ineffective in instructing them. (The opposite case, of tutors who are highly successful as instructors but ineffective as motivators, seems much rarer.)

A third preliminary observation is that our best tutors are not merely good at this job; they are superb. We have observed tutoring sessions in which students have made remarkable progress, along both cognitive and socio-emotional dimensions. In the course of a single tutoring session, students initially identified as in great need of remediation (indeed, who seemed completely unable to solve the simplest addition problems involving carrying) have progressed to solving a variety of much more complex problems (involving multiple addends, multiple and interspersed carries, verbal presentations requiring the alignment of addends of different sizes, and the like) without assistance from the tutor. Similarly, particularly low-achieving students have entered the tutoring session with heads down and eyes averted, giving every appearance of heading for the slaughterhouse—only to become transformed by the end of the session into interested, active learners who can joke with the tutor and cajole and beg him or her to provide more challenging problems.

Finally, although all of our best tutors are exquisitely sensitive and responsive to the specific actions and understandings of each individual student, there is a great deal of commonality in the general goals and strategies they display in working with the variety of tutees. And although their precise actions are highly contingent upon the actions of the student they are tutoring, our best tutors remain firmly in charge of the tutoring sessions, serving as the initiating agent in well over 90% of the exchanges that occur between tutor and tutee. One simple indicator of the general consistency in our tutors' actions with different students is shown in Figure 4-1 (on the next three pages), which displays the final "work spaces" from sessions conducted by three different tutors, each working with two students of different initial abilities.

Figure 4-1.
Sample "work spaces" from six tutoring sessions, illustrating the considerable consistency in individual tutors' approaches with different students. Each page displays the work of a different tutor—all teaching the same content—working with two students, one of high initial ability and self-confidence (the top panel) and one of low initial ability and self-confidence (the bottom panel).

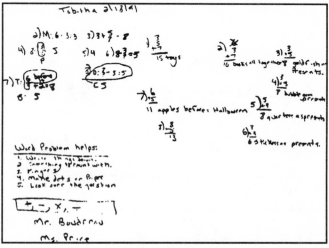

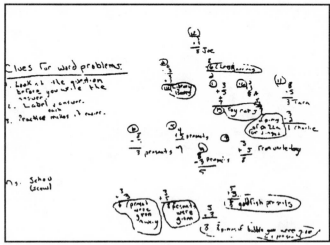

Figure 4-1 (continued).

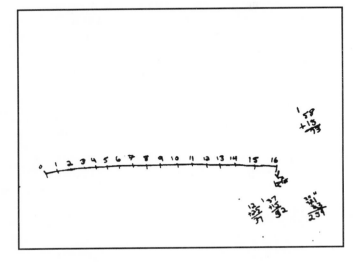

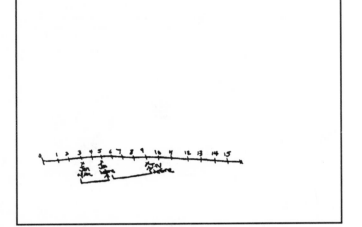

Figure 4-1 (continued).

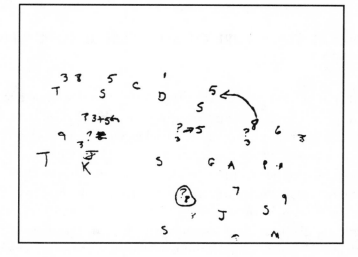

In short, our first general conclusion is that it indeed seems reasonable to proceed as we have—to identify particularly effective, expert tutors and to try to characterize the strategies and techniques that make them so successful.

GENERAL STRUCTURE OF SUCCESSFUL TUTORING SESSIONS

Another important empirical finding from our project is that effective tutoring sessions seem to share a fairly predictable "helical" structure. Because this structure provides the background for our other observations of expert tutors, it warrants a brief explanation at this point.

Basically, in the best tutoring sessions we have observed, the tutor presents a progression of increasingly difficult problems for solution by the tutee, with the tutor providing both cognitive and motivational scaffolding of the student's work when needed. For each of these problems, it is possible to identify a cycle of phases through which the tutor and tutee progress. Through the course of a tutoring session, this cycle is repeated with problems of increasing complexity, so that the progress of a successful session resembles a helix.

Problem Selection

The starting point for each problem cycle is the tutor's selection of a problem to present. At the beginning of a session, the tutor usually chooses problems designed to assess the tutee's current level of competence and to diagnose the tutee's possible misconceptions. This initial diagnosis period may be omitted if the tutor already has information about the tutee's current capabilities from prior tests or previous interactions.

Later in the session, problem selection typically depends upon the tutor's assessment of the tutee's current knowledge and current motivational state. In general, the goal here is to select problems that will prove challenging, but not impossible for the student—problems that fall, to use Vygotsky's term, within the student's "zone of proximal development" (Berk & Winsler, 1995; Vygotsky, 1962; Wertsch, 1985).

Problem Presentation

Once a problem has been selected, the tutor must decide how to present it to the student. During this presentation phase, a great deal of motivational work is accomplished (Lepper, Aspinwall, Mumme, & Chabay, 1990; Lepper, Woolverton, Mumme, & Gurtner, 1993). As a new problem is presented, our best tutors will directly challenge the student (e.g., "This is a really tough one. I don't know if you'll be able to do it. Do you think you can handle it?"). Or, occasionally, they may reassure students. In addition, the tutors may seek to enhance curiosity and to encourage reflection by posing thought-provoking questions (e.g., "Do you think that this method will produce the same result as in the previous problem?"). Sometimes, they may offer the student choices on how to proceed (e.g., "Would you rather try it this way or that way?" or "Would you like to use these [manipulatives] on this problem?"). Finally, the presentation of a new problem frequently provides tutors with an opportunity to comment upon the student's progress over the course of the tutoring session.

At the same time, during this presentation phase, good tutors often provide labels for, and information regarding, the nature of the problem to come (e.g., "Let's try a two-part word problem this time," or "Here's a type of problem you haven't seen before"). Labeling problems and problem categories has been shown in other contexts to facilitate associations between current learning and previous or future occurrences of related problems (Leinhardt, 1987, 1988). Similarly, forewarning about new or distinctive characteristics of an upcoming problem may facilitate the student's orientation to that problem.

Problem Solution

Once a problem has been presented, the tutor's central goal is to allow the student to correctly solve the problem. Occasionally, this merely involves allowing the student to proceed on his or her own. But most of the time, because our good tutors have high expectations and deliberately present challenging problems, the student will make an error or get stuck and require some sort of assistance. Therefore, the central choice points for the tutor during this solution phase concern when and how to offer assistance when the student is experiencing difficulties (e.g., Chabay & Sherwood, 1992; Lepper & Chabay, 1988; Merrill, Reiser, Merrill, & Landes, 1995).

Interestingly, in our studies with remedial students in the domain of elementary arithmetic, our best tutors seem to respond to student errors rather differently than their less effective colleagues. First, our best tutors appear to draw upon a more highly nuanced and sophisticated set of responses to different kinds of student errors. Whereas our less successful tutors are more likely to respond to student errors in some fairly standardized manner, our top tutors appear to respond differentially to different types of errors as a function of their analyses of the structure and causes of each error. Second, our best tutors seem constantly alert to the likely reoccurrence of systematic errors, or "bugs," encountered on previous problems and seem continuously vigilant for signs of anticipated errors that have not yet taken place.

In fact, although still preliminary, our initial analyses suggest that our most effective tutors show at least four distinctive responses to actual and anticipated student errors:

1. *Ignoring.* Our best tutors choose simply to ignore some errors. This response seems to occur most frequently with errors that appear inconsequential to the tutor. Typically this class includes both errors in procedure and errors in form that do not lead to errors in the actual answer reached (e.g., allowing a student to begin adding on the left for a problem that does not require carrying, or not insisting on the student's inclusion of a written "plus" sign). Less successful tutors, in contrast, are often unable to let even minor and inconsequential errors go without correction.

2. *Forestalling.* A second tactic displayed by our effective tutors

is to try to forestall (i.e., prevent the occurrence of) anticipated or clearly incipient errors when the tutor believes these are likely to disrupt the solution process. Thus, our best tutors are continuously diagnosing and monitoring underlying misconceptions or faulty algorithms—systematic "bugs" that the tutor expects to recur each time the same sort of problem arises until they have been fixed. When a particular bug has appeared in previous problems and has not yet been fixed, the effective tutor proactively looks for its recurrence on subsequent problems. Similarly, our best tutors appear constantly vigilant for subtle signs (e.g., a pencil resting above the incorrect column in an arithmetic problem, or a reading of a problem with misplaced emphasis) that suggest that the tutee is about to proceed down an incorrect path.

Anticipated or incipient errors are likely to be defined as "disruptive" when: (1) upon reconsideration of the problem, the student is unlikely to be able to identify and correct the error without extensive support by the tutor, and/or (2) the student is likely to be led down a long and incorrect "garden path" before its consequences will be appreciated. Effective tutors try to forestall these sorts of errors. They ask leading questions, or provide hints of other sorts, in order to prevent the student from making these expected errors (e.g., "Which one is the ones column?" or "Where do we start when we are adding?").

If, by contrast, the error is seen as "productive"—as one from which students might effectively learn some principle by discovering the mistake themselves—the tutor allows it to occur even when its occurrence is anticipated.

3. *Intervening.* A third common response of our expert tutors to certain sorts of errors is immediate and direct intervention. Direct interventions (e.g., "No, let's start here," or "Seventeen? Are you sure?") are intended to produce an immediate correction of the error. They appear to be used primarily in two cases. First, when an attempt to forestall a disruptive error fails, the tutor will be likely to intervene as soon as that error

has actually occurred. Here, once again, the tutor hopes to prevent these errors from disrupting the solution process. Second, our top tutors also respond with immediate interventions when an error appears to be a trivial or inadvertent mistake. Here, their aim is to prevent careless errors from distracting the student from the larger and more important lessons to be learned from the problem.

4. *Debugging.* Finally, in cases where unanticipated errors have occurred or where students have deliberately been permitted to make a particular error, our tutors engage in a process of "debugging" those errors. This process, like tutors' attempts to forestall certain errors, primarily involves the tutors' posing leading questions or offering other hints designed to prompt students to identify and correct for themselves the errors in question. Typically, these questions begin as fairly general and indirect inquiries. Should these initial inquiries fail, the tutor is likely to continue in the mode of asking questions of the student, but to do so in an increasingly direct and specific fashion. Indeed, when all less direct approaches have failed, our tutors often engage in a "stepping through" process— posing for the student a series of very specific questions that involve an entire reworking of the problem one step at a time.[2]

Reflection

After a problem has been successfully solved, our effective tutors usually (but not always) proceed to reflect upon that problem's solution or, occasionally, upon the more general progress of the tutoring session as a whole. In cognitive terms, if the solution phase is devoted primarily to acquiring procedural skills and knowledge, the reflection phase is devoted primarily to developing declarative and

---

[2] Similar "debugging modules" sometimes also appear during the reflection and presentation phases, as well as the solution phase. This happens, for example, when a student makes an error, or appears stuck, in trying to respond to a tutor's questions or requests for elaboration during these phases.

conceptual knowledge associated with the procedural skills being learned. At this point, students are often asked to provide an explanation of what they have just done on the previous problem (e.g., "Now tell me how you got that answer"). If the explanation is incomplete or incorrect, the tutor may elaborate further upon the student's comments. Or the student may be asked to make conceptual comparisons across different problems (e.g., "How was this problem different from the last problem?" or "Show me which of these problems involved [operation] and which did not"). In motivational terms, the reflection phase (along with the presentation phase) can also be a time for noting the progress the student has made, either within the session or compared to some other benchmark.

Instruction

Depending upon the nature of the tutoring sessions, one may also observe a pure instruction phase, in which the tutor offers direct instruction regarding the subject under study or provides a demonstration of how a problem should be solved. In our protocols, such phases were relatively uncommon, perhaps because our students had usually had previous instruction in and experience with the material they were being taught. In cases where entirely new material is being presented to students, such a phase would probably assume increased prominence.

INTERPLAY OF INFORMATIONAL AND MOTIVATIONAL FACTORS

Another general finding from our project concerns the simultaneous and continuous attention that successful tutors pay both to cognitive and informational factors, on the one hand, and to affective and motivational factors, on the other. Both from their actions and from their own descriptions of those actions and of the reasons underlying them, it seems clear that effective tutors share several important characteristics. They seek both to inform and to inspire students; they give roughly equal attention and weight to motivational and to informational factors during the tutoring sessions; and their decisions as tutors are based on concurrent ongoing assessments or models of the tutee's affective and cognitive states.

For a number of years, cognitive theorists concerned with the design of intelligent computer-based tutors have assigned central importance to the tutor's construction and maintenance of an accurate model of the student's understanding and misconceptions (e.g., Dede, 1986; Sleeman & Brown, 1982; Wenger, 1987). Our observations suggest that this sort of cognitive modeling also plays an important part in determining the responses of our expert tutors, although their attempts to "diagnose" and categorize systematic student errors are less detailed and complex than those built into most computer-based diagnostic modeling systems (e.g., Larkin & Chabay, 1992; Sleeman, Kelly, Martinak, Ward, & Moore, 1989).

At the same time, however, our observations suggest that expert human tutors show an equal concern for a variety of social, affective, and motivational factors that are not considered in most computer-based tutoring systems. In particular, our best tutors seem to have motivational goals of at least four general types, as discussed in greater detail by Lepper et al. (1993):

1. *Confidence.* Perhaps the most important and prevalent motivational goal of our expert tutors is the enhancement of students' feelings of self-confidence and self-esteem. This seems especially important for remedial students who have a history of difficulty with the subject at hand and begin the tutoring sessions with low self-esteem and little confidence in their abilities.

2. *Challenge.* While our expert tutors seek to enhance students' self-esteem and confidence, they do not "dumb down" the material, concentrating on problems so simple they know the student will be able to succeed at them. It is equally important for expert tutors that the child feel challenged. In fact, our best

tutors often emphasize the challenging nature of, and the accompanying possibility of failure at, the problems they have provided.

3. *Curiosity.* Our best tutors also seek to create situations that will heighten students' curiosity about the material under study, to lead their tutees to become more actively involved in the subject matter at hand.

4. *Control.* Finally, our most effective tutors work hard to instill in their pupils a sense of control and self-efficacy. Because the very nature of a tutorial could easily make the learner feel externally controlled and resistant, good tutors take special care to encourage in students a sense of efficacy and control.[3]

With the above motivational goals—as with the tutors' more evident informational and cognitive goals—expert tutors hope to produce changes that will persist beyond the immediate tutoring session. Just as they hope their students' gains in knowledge will be evident at home or in their classrooms long after the tutoring sessions have ended, these tutors want to cultivate a sense of self-confidence, challenge, curiosity, and control that will influence their students' approach to further relevant learning opportunities—especially in future settings where the tutor will no longer be present.

We believe that it makes sense to think of effective human tutors as constructing and maintaining a diagnostic model of the student's affective and motivational state—just as they do of the student's state of knowledge and understanding—during the tutoring session (Derry, 1989; Derry, Hawkes, & Tsai, 1987). We have found it useful to analyze many of the tutor's most important decisions, such as what problem to give next or how to respond to a particular student error, in terms of their simultaneous attention to the student's informational and motivational states. In fact, when trying to predict in a

---

[3] Yet another general goal of motivational, as well as potential cognitive, significance involves the *contextualization* of instruction—i.e., the presentation of abstract material within real or imagined concrete settings that provide an interesting and meaningful context for learning and application (e.g., Cordova & Lepper, 1995; Parker & Lepper, 1992).

given situation what a particular tutor might do next, it is often helpful to postulate that he or she begins with two separate sorts of questions: *purely cognitive questions* (e.g., How might I most efficiently transmit new information to correct this learner's misunderstandings or augment that learner's knowledge?), and *purely affective questions* (e.g., How might I most effectively bolster this student's self-confidence or heighten that student's sense of control?). Decisions about how the tutor should proceed at any point can be seen to depend upon the answers to both types of questions, and upon the relationship between these answers—a relationship that may take one of three general forms.

First, in many cases, the next steps suggested by a purely cognitive analysis and by a purely motivational analysis will prove highly consistent and mutually supportive. For example, if a tutor is trying to determine what sort of problem to present to a student who has just solved several problems at a given level of difficulty without assistance, both cognitive and motivational analyses may suggest the same action: presenting a new problem of somewhat greater difficulty. In these cases, the tutor's next step appears to be overdetermined, and even less effective tutors may routinely reach the same conclusion.

In other situations, the cognitive and the motivational analyses may simply prove independent of one another. A motivational analysis, for example, might suggest that it is useful for a tutor to attribute successes to the student (e.g., "You got that one all by yourself"), but to attribute failures to the tutor (e.g., "I guess I made that problem too difficult, didn't I?"), the dyad (e.g., "We're really stumped on this one, aren't we?"), or even "outside" forces (e.g., "They've really given us a tough one this time"); whereas a cognitive analysis would be moot on that particular point. Conversely, a cognitive analysis will often suggest substantive material, about which a motivational analysis would have nothing to say.

Finally, and most interestingly, a purely cognitive and a purely motivational analysis may work at cross-purposes to one another and may yield competing plans for action. From a purely cognitive perspective, for example, the most direct response to a student error reflecting a deep conceptual misunderstanding may be to inform the student that the answer is incorrect and to provide the correct answer, perhaps adding an explicit analysis of precisely where the student went wrong. Yet this seemingly efficient informational communication is often contraindicated by a motivational analysis. From an affective perspective, such direct negative feedback may be likely to further undermine motivation and self-confidence, at least for students with a history of failure and low self-esteem. In cases of conflicting pressures, as we shall see shortly, our best tutors utilize a variety of strategies for correcting errors indirectly, so as not to undermine the student's sense of self-confidence or personal control.

As we examine the more specific strategies and techniques of our most effective tutors, we will need to be constantly alert to these tutors' simultaneous concerns with affective and cognitive goals and considerations and to the strategies that balance both. In fact, although it is possible to analyze affective and cognitive considerations separately, the vast majority of a good tutor's actions and remarks seem designed to simultaneously serve both motivational and informational functions. In short, the scaffolding that expert tutors provide to enhance students' performance involves both affective and cognitive supports.

CHARACTERISTICS & STRATEGIES OF SUCCESSFUL TUTORS: HOW TUTORS "INSPIRE" LEARNING

How, then, are the general goals of our successful tutors translated into specific actions? What is it that our most effective tutors actually do to scaffold learning and to produce such remarkable cognitive and motivational gains in students?

We have found the acronym "INSPIRE" to provide a useful summary of several salient strategies and characteristics displayed by our expert tutors. The basic elements included in this acronym are displayed in Figure 4-2 on the next page. Let us examine each of these constituent elements, in turn, in greater detail.

Figure 4-2.
INSPIRE as an acronym for summarizing the techniques and
characteristics of expert tutors.

Intelligent
Nurturant
Socratic
Progressive
Indirect
Reflective
Encouraging

Intelligent

One of the foremost characteristics of our expert tutors is the amount
of intelligence or knowledge they bring to the tutoring situation.
Indeed, our best tutors show higher levels of knowledge, of several
different sorts, than their less effective counterparts (Shulman, 1987).

First, our most effective tutors seem to have much more knowledge of the relevant subject matter than do our less effective tutors.
Although this is not, in general, an unexpected finding, we did find
ourselves surprised on two counts. Since the tutoring involved very
simple material, such as basic addition and subtraction, we had
expected any experienced teacher to have well beyond the required
level of expertise. Yet differences in subject-matter knowledge were
nonetheless evident, even though all tutors were very familiar with
this domain. Also somewhat surprising was the range of related
subjects that our tutors occasionally draw upon. To take but one
salient example, we found ourselves quite struck when a fourth-grade
boy's trouble with fractions led his tutor to expound upon the ancient
Egyptians and the difficulties *they* had had, despite their great engin-

eering successes, with fractions.

In addition to their general subject knowledge, our expert tutors also seem particularly well versed in what might be called *subject-specific pedagogical knowledge*. Our best tutors typically know, for instance, which problems will look more difficult to students than they really are, and which problems will look less difficult than they really are. Indeed, these tutors have a shared "technical term"— "tricky"—that they use when introducing problems of this latter sort. Our most effective tutors also appear to draw from a wide repertoire of analogies and metaphors to help explain or illustrate difficult concepts. When faced with the prospect of explaining negative numbers to a student for the first time, a good tutor may illustrate the concept with reference to the weather and temperatures below zero; or to financial accounts and the meaning of debits and credits; or to the "negative" space left when a bucket of sand is removed from the beach; or to formal mathematical devices, such as a number line.

Finally, our expert tutors also appear to excel in more general pedagogical knowledge. In this last category falls these tutors' knowledge of effective strategies both for instructing and for motivating students—knowledge, for example, of the sorts of general techniques already discussed in previous sections.

Nurturant

While the preceding comments tend to emphasize the cognitive side of tutoring, our expert tutors simultaneously display a high level of affective support and nurturance in their interactions with students. This is reflected in a number of ways.

At the outset of the tutoring sessions, our best tutors appear to spend more time than other tutors building rapport with their tutees. They inquire about the student's home and school, and often about favorite sports, hobbies, or movies, as well as about their backgrounds in math. Often, these tutors continue to refer to personal information about the student (e.g., the student's classroom teacher or a favorite participatory sport) during the course of the session.

In addition, compared to less effective tutors, our most effective tutors seem to be much more attentive to their students. As mentioned earlier, our best tutors are continuously vigilant regarding their students' work, with the result that potentially disruptive errors can often be forestalled or nipped in the bud. Expert tutors also seem more attentive to the emotional state of their tutees. As a result, they are able to recognize and intervene earlier when the student is clearly stuck, but unwilling or unable to say so directly, and they are aware when the student appears to be particularly anxious or discouraged.

Moreover, these tutors seem to display a high level of empathy for the difficulties that their students experience. In fact, they often take remarkable pains to keep especially low-achieving students from feeling like failures. These tutors often forewarn students when a particularly difficult problem is presented. Such forewarning allows students to feel less sting should they have difficulty, since, after all, it *was* a very hard problem. We can be certain that such labels often serve motivational goals, because tutors sometimes misrepresent the difficulty of a problem when they feel that the student is becoming unduly discouraged or frustrated. Sometimes these tutors take responsibility for a pupil's errors, claiming, for example, that they had probably not explained the problem clearly or had selected too difficult a challenge. Likewise, they may commiserate with the student by recalling how much trouble they themselves had when they first encountered this subject. Often, they even find ways to transform evident failures into at least partial successes (e.g., "Well, that's exactly right, *if* we had been trying to solve *that* problem," or even "Perfect! Except that you missed it").

Finally, we should note that our best tutors also show a high level of interest and enthusiasm for their students. These tutors, we believe, share what Dweck (Dweck, 1986; Dweck & Leggett, 1988) would call an "incremental" theory of performance; they believe that any student can be helped to learn. More generally, they enjoy this sort of work, and it shows.

Socratic

A third prominent characteristic of our expert tutors is their reliance on, and commitment to, a fundamentally Socratic style of tutoring (Collins & Stevens, 1982; Stevens, Collins, & Goldin, 1982). Along a variety of dimensions, these tutors seek to draw as much as possible out of their students and to make learning an active and constructive process. There are several aspects to this style.

First, our best tutors rely enormously on questions, rather than statements or directions. We have already noted, for example, their tendency to use leading questions to try to forestall or to debug student errors. More generally, we find that 80–90% of an expert tutor's total remarks during an average tutoring session are in the form of questions, with only 5% in the form of directions. Our best tutors, in short, greatly prefer asking to telling.

Particularly when working with remedial students, our top tutors are quite committed to this questioning strategy. Even when it takes a series of six or eight leading questions before the student grasps a point, these tutors persist in posing questions rather than issuing directives. An observer who did not know that these tutors had produced such excellent results might be tempted to dismiss their strategy as highly inefficient, and to suggest that they ought instead to be telling the student directly exactly what needs to be done.

Our conversations with these tutors suggest at least two reasons for their persistence in this Socratic tutoring style. On the one hand, these tutors believe that hints and questions promote a more active involvement from the student that is likely to enhance retention of the material learned. On the other, this strategy appears to strike a compromise between cognitive and affective considerations. That is, these tutors feel that the most efficient means of directly transmitting corrective feedback (e.g., "That is incorrect. Here is the right answer, and here is where you went wrong ...") often has strong detrimental effects on students' self-confidence and subsequent motivation. Their Socratic technique is intended, in part, as a strategy for conveying needed informative and corrective feedback, while minimizing the negative emotional consequences that such feedback might have for learners low in self-confidence.

Progressive

A fourth characteristic of our expert tutors is their commitment to make increasing demands on the student in each tutoring session. Despite their general reluctance to convey direct negative feedback to students, these tutors are not undemanding of their students; they are actually quite the opposite. Our best tutors have high aspirations for their tutees. They demand attention and effort from their students, and they expect to see visible progress within each tutoring session.

This commitment to progress is evident at several different levels. First, one sees a systematic progression built into the sequences of problems presented by our best tutors. In general, each time the student succeeds at one problem without assistance, the tutor is likely to select a next problem at a slightly higher level of difficulty. When the student has difficulties with a particular problem, the tutor is likely to offer another problem at that same level, and perhaps to give some additional assistance. By contrast, even though this perhaps seems such a simple idea, our less effective tutors often present problems in a non-systematic (i.e., haphazard) manner, or in a systematic but non-progressive (i.e., cyclical) manner in which successive problems do not necessarily build upon one another or depend greatly upon the student's previous performance.

Our best tutors also use progressive strategies when debugging an incorrect response. They appear to use a variant of the specific scaffolding strategy first described by Wood and Middleton (1975). When first responding to a student error, the tutor is likely to pose a question or offer a hint at a fairly general and unconstrained level (e.g., "Where do we start when we add?"). If the student responds incorrectly, the tutor's questions are likely to become increasingly specific and constrained (e.g., "Which one is the ones column?") until the student responds correctly. On the other hand, once the student provides a correct answer, the tutor's questions will quickly revert to a much more general level. As a result, across problems of a given sort, the tutor will offer progressively less assistance and will expect progressively more from the student.

Generally, we find that our best tutors are more likely than their less successful counterparts to establish and follow clear routines within a tutoring session. It is, for example, much easier for judges analyzing their protocols to identify shifts from one phase to another (e.g., from presentation to solution to reflection), and it is easier for judges to describe these tutors' particular patterns for providing feedback, presenting problems, or offering reflections to the student.

Indirect

While our most effective tutors seem highly demanding of students, they convey their high expectations in a very indirect and unprepossessing manner. At least when working with remedial students, our good tutors are polite and unobtrusive, practically to a fault.

This indirect style is perhaps most apparent in the types of negative feedback employed by these tutors. It is striking in our protocols how seldom these tutors provide direct negative feedback, such as telling the student directly that an answer is wrong, giving the student the correct answer, pointing out where the student went wrong, or explicitly demonstrating how the problem should be solved. More often, negative feedback takes the form of relatively indirect hints that clearly *imply* that something is wrong, but stop short of saying so directly (e.g., "So how did you get that 6?" or "Which numbers did you really want to use?" or "O.K. So how many presents all together?"). As noted above, these tutors' attempts to forestall certain sorts of errors show comparable indirectness.

A similar, but somewhat less obvious, subtlety can also be seen in

---

4   It is important to note, however, that the apparent subtlety of these distinctions between indirect positive and negative feedback does not lead to confusion on the part of students. In this example, for instance, the child responded to the "negative" comment by immediately erasing the "6," but responded to the "positive" comment by beginning to offer an explanation of where the "2" had come from.

these top tutors' attribution strategies. Rather than directly attributing the students' successes to their efforts and abilities and their failures to external factors—a strategy suggested by a number of formal studies of what has been called "attribution retraining" (Dweck, 1975; Foersterling, 1985)—these tutors are likely to present new problems with the periodic caveat that they are perhaps too difficult for the student. As a result, students can draw their own conclusions: If they succeed at these difficult tasks, they can feel proud of their success; but should they fail at such difficult challenges, they can easily attribute their failure to the unreasonable demands of the task. When used with remedial students, this indirect strategy has been shown experimentally to produce more beneficial motivational effects than the other well-tested attribution retraining procedures (Lepper et al., 1990).

Even when offering positive feedback, our best tutors often use an indirect style. The correct solution to a problem may be met with a simple statement that merely implies that the student's answer was correct (e.g., "Well, let's go on to a more difficult one," or "Let's try a different type of problem."). In the extreme, except for subtleties of intonation and phrasing, some statements following correct solutions seem almost indistinguishable from statements following incorrect solutions (e.g., contrast one tutor's negative feedback in the form, "So how did you get that 6?" versus positive feedback in the form, "So tell me how you got that 2?"). Conversely, it is often our least effective tutors who seem to bubble over with effusive praise whenever the student makes the slightest progress.[4]

Reflective

A sixth characteristic of our expert tutors is their high level of reflection, compared to our less effective tutors. These tutors are more likely to articulate, and especially to encourage and help the student to articulate, the reasoning and meaning underlying the mathematical operations being taught. For example, following the correct solution of a problem, these tutors are likely to ask students to explain their strategies or to summarize their problem-solving process (e.g., "Now tell me what you were doing here," or "And how did you arrive at that answer?"). In addition, if the tutee provides an accurate but incomplete explanation, these tutors are likely to provide a recast or expansion of the student's explanation (Nelson, 1987, 1989).

In other cases, students are asked during the reflection phase to generalize their work to some real-world context or to compare or contrast the problem they just solved to previously undertaken problems. Often, our best tutors deliberately plan their presentation of problems to facilitate the asking of thought-provoking questions that involve the comparison of different problems or problem-solving techniques (e.g., "If you now do the same problem in this different way, will you get the same answer, or a different one?").

During the reflection phase, also, some expert tutors periodically asked their students to describe in their own words, or even to write down, the general lessons that they might have learned from working through the last problem or set of problems. Students' immediate responses, which often focus on very specific aspects of the problem, are then progressively shaped—via further questions from the tutor—into general "lessons" that are not specific to a particular problem or problem type, but are still in the student's own words.

Such self-generated explanations and lessons, these tutors believe, have considerable value in helping students to generalize and apply their knowledge to subsequent related problems. Some studies on learning phenomena associated with the "generation effect" and the "self-reference effect" provide data consistent with this belief (e.g., Chi, deLeeuw, Chiu, & LaVancher, 1994; Foos, Mora, & Tkacz, 1994). At the least, such techniques should guarantee that students will be able to associate the relevant underlying concepts with the algorithms and procedures they have learned.

Encouraging

Finally, our top tutors clearly devote a great deal of effort to encouraging or motivating students, not just to work hard, but to enjoy their work and to feel challenged, empowered, and curious about the domain under study. As noted earlier in this chapter and discussed in more detail by Lepper et al. (1990), we see clear evidence that good tutors seek to promote the learner's sense of self-confidence, challenge, curiosity, and control.

To bolster self-confidence, for instance, expert tutors regularly minimize their students' failures (e.g., by commiserating, reassuring, making excuses, or redefining goals) and maximize their successes (e.g., by expressing confidence, emphasizing student agency, and engaging in playful competition with the students). To maintain a sense of challenge, successful tutors constantly modulate both the objective difficulty of the task (either through the selection of problems presented or through provision of assistance and scaffolding during the solution process) and the subjective difficulty of the task (either through direct and playful challenges to the student, or by explicitly labeling the task as more or less difficult).

To provoke a sense of curiosity, these tutors rely on the Socratic questioning strategy mentioned above and seek to associate materials to be learned with topics, themes, and characters of particular interest to the student. Finally, to promote a sense of control, these tutors attempt to increase both the student's level of actual control (by offering choices, complying with reasonable student requests, and transferring control to the student) and the student's level of perceived control (by emphasizing student agency, promoting illusions of control, and employing indirect forms of feedback and direction).

These various techniques, our tutors hope, will not only produce short-term benefits, in terms of performance during the tutoring sessions, but also lead to long-term increases in students' motivation that should persist well after the conclusion of the tutoring sessions (Malone & Lepper, 1987; Lepper & Malone, 1987).

DISCUSSION

In the foregoing sections, we have tried to provide a thumbnail sketch of some of the general goals and the specific strategies and techniques used by expert human tutors to provide both instructional and motivational scaffolding for students. In this final section, we briefly consider some potential limitations and potential applications of our findings and analyses.

Qualifications

There are, of course, many qualifications that might be placed on these preliminary conclusions about the determinants of successful tutoring. Our studies have obviously focused on students in a particular age range, primarily from first through sixth grades; they have concentrated, moreover, on the domain of elementary mathematics; and so forth. Of the many potential limitations on our findings, we believe that the following are the most critical.

First, it seems of paramount importance to emphasize that our tutors are working with a captive audience, rather than with students who have sought out tutoring to improve their skills or performance in some domain of personal interest or concern. Second, it also seems crucial to emphasize that most of the students in our tutoring sessions initially had low self-confidence and high anxiety about their competence at the task. Although we have not yet investigated these issues, we hypothesize that tutors working with more highly motivated and more highly confident students have considerably more latitude to provide direct instruction, to offer explicit feedback, and to be at least somewhat less focused upon students' feelings of self-esteem and competence.

On the other hand, judging from recent analyses (e.g., Steele, 1992, 1995; Steele & Aronson, 1995), minority students or otherwise stigmatized students may have particular difficulties and concerns in these sorts of potentially evaluative situations. Therefore, motivational and affective concerns may assume greater prominence with such students.

Applications

Despite these qualifications, it is worth noting the potential relevance of our findings to a variety of settings, beyond those in which every student has the singular luxury of working individually with an expert tutor. In recent years, for example, many schools have sought to augment traditional classroom instruction with various paraprofessional volunteers who serve as individual tutors for remedial students. Other schools have sought to enhance instruction and foster increased parental involvement by designing formal programs to encourage parental tutoring of students. In both of these cases, we suggest, useful lessons about tutor training may be learned from our examinations of the goals and strategies of experts in this field.[5]

Similarly, the present study may have implications for training students as tutors in cross-age or peer-tutoring programs. In fact, it would be of interest to study directly the dynamics of effective peer tutoring programs. Obviously, the developmental literature implies that there are many aspects of our expert tutors' performance that peer tutors are not likely to display. However, there is overwhelming evidence of the effectiveness of such programs despite these "deficiencies" (Levin, Glass, & Meister, 1984).

Much less clear in practice, but perhaps of greatest theoretical interest, is the relevance of the current studies to the design of effective computer-based tutors. Certainly, we do not assume that computer tutors should be patterned after their human counterparts. Computers clearly afford pedagogical opportunities that even expert tutors cannot match (see Lajoie & Derry, 1993; Larkin & Chabay, 1992); clearly, too, there are also still important ways in which current computers cannot mimic humans (see Lepper & Chabay, 1988).

---

[5] In addition, individual professional tutoring is a key element in a number of recent school-reform programs, such as Clay's (1985, 1991) increasingly popular "Reading Recovery" programs.

Nonetheless, it seems a potentially rich and fascinating problem for future research to ask what import the study of human experts in this domain might have for the design of computer tutors (see Merrill et al., 1995).

POSTSCRIPT

In seeking to identify and describe the goals and strategies used by expert human tutors to scaffold student learning and motivation, we have searched periodically for a metaphor that aptly describes the role of the tutor in the protocols we have analyzed. In the end, we have been drawn back to George Polya's famous dictum on teaching—that teachers should be "midwives" to "ideas born in the students' minds"—as a description of the subtle, respectful, indirect, Socratic style of our expert tutors.

REFERENCES

Berk, L.E., & Winsler, A. (1995). *Scaffolding children's learning: Vygotsky and early childhood education.* Washington, DC: National Association for the Education of Young Children.

Bloom, B.S. (1984). The 2-sigma problem: The search for methods of group instruction as effective as one-to-one tutoring. *Educational Researcher, 13,* 4-16.

Chabay, R.W., & Sherwood, B.A. (1992). A practical guide for the creation of educational software. In J.H. Larkin & R.W. Chabay (Eds.), *Computer-assisted instruction and intelligent tutoring systems: Shared goals and complementary approaches* (pp. 151-186). Hillsdale, NJ: Erlbaum.

Chi, M.T.H., deLeeuw, N., Chiu, M-H., & LaVancher, C. (1994). Eliciting self-explanations improves understanding. *Cognitive Science, 18,* 439-477.

Clay, M.M. (1985). *The early detection of reading difficulties.* Portsmouth, NH: Heinemann.

Clay, M.M. (1991). *Becoming literate: The construction of inner control.* Portsmouth, NH: Heinemann.

Collins, A., & Stevens, A.L. (1982). Goals and strategies of inquiry teachers. In

R. Glaser (Ed.), *Advances in instructional psychology* (Vol. 2, pp. 65-119). Hillsdale, NJ: Erlbaum.

Cordova, D.I., & Lepper, M.R. (in press). Intrinsic motivation and the process of learning: Beneficial effects of contextualization, personalization, and choice. *Journal of Educational Psychology.*

Dede, C.J. (1986). A review and synthesis of recent research in intelligent computer-assisted instruction. *International Journal of Man-Machine Studies, 24,* 329-353.

Derry, S.J. (1989). Strategy and expertise in word problem solving. In C. McCormick, G. Miller, & M. Pressley (Eds.), *Cognitive strategy research: From basic research to educational applications* (pp. 269-302). New York: Springer-Verlag.

Derry, S.J., Hawkes, L.W., & Tsai, C. (1987). A theory for remediating problem-solving skills of older children and adults. *Educational Psychologist, 22,* 55-87.

Dweck, C.S. (1975). The role of expectations and attributions in the alleviation of learned helplessness. *Journal of Personality and Social Psychology, 31,* 674-685.

Dweck, C.S. (1986). Motivational processes affecting learning. *American Psychologist, 41,* 1040-1048.

Dweck, C.S., & Leggett, E.L. (1988). A social-cognitive approach to motivation and personality. *Psychological Review, 95,* 256-273.

Foersterling, F. (1985). Attributional retraining: A review. *Psychological Bulletin, 98,* 495-512.

Foos, P.W., Mora, J.J., & Tkacz, S. (1994). Student study techniques and the generation effect. *Journal of Educational Psychology, 86,* 567-576.

Lajoie, S.P., & Derry, S.J. (Eds.). (1993). *Computers as cognitive tools.* Hillsdale, NJ: Erlbaum.

Larkin, J.H., & Chabay, R.W. (Eds.). (1992). *Computer-assisted instruction and intelligent tutoring systems: Shared goals and complementary approaches.* Hillsdale, NJ: Erlbaum.

Leinhardt, G. (1987). Development of an expert explanation: An analysis of a sequence of subtraction lessons. *Cognition and Instruction, 4,* 225-282.

Leinhardt, G. (1988). Expertise in instructional lessons: An example from fractions. In D.A. Grouws & R.J. Cooney (Eds.), *Perspectives on research on effective mathematics teaching* (pp. 47-66). Hillsdale, NJ: Erlbaum.

Lepper, M.R., Aspinwall, L.G., Mumme, D.L., & Chabay, R.W. (1990). Self-perception and social-perception processes in tutoring: Subtle social control strategies of expert tutors. In J.M. Olson & M.P. Zanna (Eds.), *Self-inference processes: The Ontario symposium* (pp. 217-237). Hillsdale, NJ: Erlbaum.

Lepper, M.R., & Chabay, R.W. (1988). Socializing the intelligent tutor: Bringing empathy to computer tutors. In H. Mandl & A.M. Lesgold (Eds.), *Learning issues for intelligent tutoring systems* (pp. 242-257). Chicago: Springer-Verlag.

Lepper, M.R., & Malone, T.W. (1987). Intrinsic motivation and instructional effectiveness in computer-based education. In R.E. Snow & M.J. Farr (Eds.), *Aptitude, learning, and instruction: III. Conative and affective process analyses* (pp. 255-296). Hillsdale, NJ: Erlbaum.

Lepper, M.R., Woolverton, M., Mumme, D.L., & Gurtner, J-L. (1993). Motivational techniques of expert human tutors: Lessons for the design of computer-based tutors. In S.P. Lajoie & S.J. Derry (Eds.), *Computers as cognitive tools* (pp. 75-105). Hillsdale, NJ: Erlbaum.

Levin, H.M., Glass, E., & Meister, G. (1984). *A cost-effectiveness analysis of four educational interventions.* IFG Project Report No. 84-A11. Stanford, CA: Institute for Research on Educational Finance and Governance.

Malone, T.W., & Lepper, M.R. (1987). Making learning fun: A taxonomy of intrinsic motivations for learning. In R.E. Snow & M.J. Farr (Eds.),*Aptitude, learning, and instruction: III. Conative and affective process analyses* (pp. 223-253). Hillsdale, NJ: Erlbaum.

Merrill, D.C., Reiser, B.J., Merrill, S.K., & Landes, S. (1995). Tutoring: Guided learning by doing. *Cognition and Instruction, 13,* 315-372.

Nelson, K.E. (1987). Some observations from the perspective of the rare event cognitive comparison theory of language acquisition. In K.E. Nelson (Ed.), *Children's language,* Vol. 6. Hillsdale, NJ: Erlbaum.

Nelson, K.E. (1989). Strategies for first language teaching. In M.L. Rice & R.L. Schiefelbusch (Eds.), *The teachability of language* (pp. 263-310). Baltimore, MD: Paul H. Brookes.

Parker, L.E., & Lepper, M.R. (1992). Effects of fantasy contexts on children's learning and motivation: Making learning more fun. *Journal of Personality and Social Psychology, 62,* 625-633.

Shulman, L.S. (1987). Knowledge and teaching: Foundations of the new reform. *Harvard Educational Review, 57,* 1-22.

Sleeman, D., & Brown, J.S. (Eds.). (1982). *Intelligent tutoring systems.* New York: Academic Press.

Sleeman, D., Kelly, A.E., Martinak, R., Ward, R.D., & Moore, J.L. (1989). Studies of diagnosis and remediation with high school algebra students. *Cognitive Science, 13,* 551-568.

Steele, C.M. (1992, April). Race and the schooling of black Americans. *The Atlantic Monthly,* 68-78.

Steele, C.M. (in press). A burden of suspicion: How stereotypes shape the intellectual identities and performance of women and African-Americans. *American Psychologist.*

Steele, C.M., & Aronson, J. (1995). Stereotype threat and the intellectual test performance of African Americans. *Journal of Personality and Social Psychol-*

ogy, 69, 797- 811.

Stevens, A., Collins, A., & Goldin, S.E. (1982). Misconceptions in students' understanding. In D. Sleeman & J.S. Brown (Eds.), *Intelligent tutoring systems* (pp. 13-24). New York: Academic Press.

Vygotsky, L.S. (1962). *Thought and language.* Cambridge, MA: MIT Press.

Wenger, E. (1987). *Artificial intelligence and tutoring systems.* Los Altos, CA: Morgan Kaufmann.

Wertsch, J.V. (1985). *Vygotsky and the social formation of mind.* Cambridge, MA: Harvard University Press.

Wood, D.J., Bruner, J.S., & Ross, G. (1976). The role of tutoring in problem solving. *Journal of Child Psychology and Psychiatry, 17,* 89-100.

Wood, D.J., & Middleton, D.J. (1975). A study of assisted problem-solving. *British Journal of Psychology, 66,* 181-191.

Wood, D.J., Wood, H.A., & Middleton, D.J. (1978). An experimental evaluation of four face-to-face teaching strategies. *International Journal of Behavioral Development, 2,* 131-147.

CHAPTER FIVE

An Anatomy of Naturalistic Tutoring

ARTHUR C. GRAESSER, CHERYL BOWERS,
& DOUGLAS J. HACKER, The University of Memphis

NATALIE PERSON, Rhodes College

One of the central challenges that classroom teachers face is the fact that students differ in knowledge, motivation, and socialization. These differences among students make it impossible to prepare a perfect lecture that optimizes learning for all of the students in the classroom. It is impossible for one teacher to handle 30 curious students simultaneously asking questions. The staging of classroom discussions is difficult when some students are passionately engaged in the issues, but others are left pie-eyed.

Fortunately, most classroom teachers find ways to minimize these obstacles as they develop their curricula and their styles of orchestrating classroom talk. However, the challenges inherent in classroom settings have inspired some educators to explore individualized student instruction, such as computer-assisted instruction, intelligent tutoring systems, and one-to-one tutoring.

When a student is having major problems learning a particular skill or specific lessons in a course, the teacher frequently assigns the

This research was funded by the Office of Naval Research (N00014-90-J-1492, and N00014-92-J-1826) and the Center for Applied Psychological Research at the University of Memphis. Queries should be sent to Arthur C. Graesser, Department of Psychology, The University of Memphis, Memphis, TN 38152.

student to a tutor. The tutor is rarely highly skilled or accomplished. The vast majority of tutors have a modest amount of domain knowledge, very little training on effective tutoring techniques, and minimal tutoring experience (Fitz-Gibbon, 1977). The tutor is typically a peer of the student having problems, a slightly older student, or a paraprofessional who tutors for money. The typical tutor for a K–12 student has had approximately nine hours of previous tutoring experience and no formal training in effective tutoring (Graesser & Person, 1994). The typical tutor for a college student has had only one or two courses on the topic being tutored and no training on tutoring skills. In many cases, the tutor is the first person the teacher manages to locate who knows a little bit about the material and who is willing to give a few hours of time to make a few extra bucks.

One of the fascinating facts about tutoring is that these "normal" unskilled tutors are extremely effective. It is well documented that students learn much more about specific lessons and skills from tutoring experiences than they do from traditional classroom activities (Anderson, Corbett, Koedinger, & Pelletier, 1995; Bloom, 1984; Cohen, Kulik, & Kulik, 1982; Mohan, 1972). The impact of unskilled tutors on student learning is not particularly sensitive to the amount of tutor training or to age differences between the tutor and student (Cohen et al., 1982). These latter findings must be tempered by the fact that the amount of tutor training and domain expertise was small. Nevertheless, the bottom line is that normal unskilled tutors are quite impressive in promoting learning in students who have experienced learning difficulties.

The primary goal of this chapter is to explore the possible reasons why normal unskilled tutors are so effective. In light of the available evidence, we will take it as fact that normal unskilled tutors are comparatively effective in promoting learning gains when specific skills and knowledge need to be acquired. Given this fact, some obvious questions immediately arise. What activities frequently occur during tutoring? Which of these activities are responsible for the advantages of tutoring? Can some of the tutors' discourse strategies in tutorial dialogue be transported into classroom settings?

This chapter will directly address the activities that occur during tutoring. In essence, we will dissect the anatomy of naturalistic tutoring, assessing the extent to which naturalistic tutoring contains a number of different components (strategies, processes, or mechanisms) that allegedly facilitate learning. These components include active student learning, use of examples, curriculum scripts, question answering, deep explanatory reasoning, feedback, error diagnosis and repair, convergence toward shared meanings, collaboration, and various sophisticated pedagogical techniques. If a particular pedagogical component is virtually absent in naturalistic tutoring, then we can conclude that the component *is not* responsible for the advantages of tutoring over the classroom. Similarly, if the incidence of a particular component is equivalent in tutoring and the classroom, then that component *is not* responsible for the advantages of tutoring. However, if a component is prevalent in tutoring and also more frequent in tutoring than in the classroom, then the component *is* a good candidate for explaining the effectiveness of tutoring. Our goal is to narrow the set of possible pedagogical mechanisms that might explain the effectiveness of tutoring. Future research can determine which of these mechanisms are actually responsible for the effectiveness of tutoring. It can also assess whether it is feasible to transport these strategies and mechanisms to classroom contexts.

Our secondary goal in this chapter is to speculate on the possibility of implementing normal tutoring techniques on a computer. Educators have frequently had the vision of having computers tutor students on skills and domain knowledge. Whereas human tutors eventually become fatigued and sometimes experience burnout, a computer tutor never gets tired. Some students are reluctant to expose their ignorance to a human tutor, but not to a computer tutor. Students report that they are more motivated to learn on an intelligent tutoring system than from a teacher, even though the students believe they would learn more from the teacher (Schofield, Eurich-Fulcer, & Britt, 1994). During the last 15 years, researchers in cognitive science have designed several intelligent tutoring systems that implement ideal pedagogical techniques. The most successful intelligent tutoring systems include Anderson's tutors for geometry, algebra, and computer languages (Anderson et al., 1995), VanLehn's tutor for basic mathematics (VanLehn, 1990), and Lesgold's tutor for diagnosing and repairing electronic equipment (Lesgold, Lajoie, Bunzo, & Eggan, 1992). Whereas these computer systems implement ideal tutoring strategies, the question arises whether it would be possible to simulate the normal unskilled tutor.

A skeptic might wonder why we would bother simulating a normal unskilled tutor when there are more ideal intelligent tutoring systems available. We have two reasons for attempting to simulate an unskilled tutor. The first reason is practical. It is extremely difficult to develop an intelligent tutoring system that has many of the powerful components that these systems attempt to deliver: modeling the idiosyncratic knowledge of a student, diagnosing and repairing the student's "bugs" and misconceptions, interpreting the language and actions of a student, and dynamically preparing lessons, explanations, and example problems that cater to the knowledge of a particular student. Given that intelligent tutoring systems are extremely difficult or impossible to build, perhaps it would be more manageable to develop a computerized tutoring system that simulates a normal unskilled tutor. The second reason for simulating a normal unskilled tutor is methodological. One way of achieving a deep understanding of a phenomenon is to simulate the phenomenon on a computer. If we could simulate the normal unskilled tutor on a computer, then we would have achieved a deep, detailed, and well-specified understanding of a normal tutor.

TWO SAMPLES OF NATURALISTIC TUTORING

In a three-year project funded by the Office of Naval Research, the authors analyzed the dialogue patterns and pedagogical components in two samples of naturalistic tutoring. In one sample, three graduate students tutored 27 undergraduate students on troublesome topics in a research methods course. The students in this sample were tutored as part of a course requirement, so there was a full range of student achievement (i.e., not just underachievement). In the other sample, 10 high school students tutored 13 seventh graders who were having major problems with particular topics in their mathematics course. The teachers had recommended tutoring to assist these students in mastering their deficits in mathematics skills. This was a bona fide corpus of naturalistic tutoring because it included all tutoring sessions on mathematics for seventh graders during a one-month period in a middle school. The tutors in both samples had a modest amount of domain knowledge, no formal training in tutoring techniques, and very little previous tutoring experience (nine hours, on the average). Thus, the tutors fit the typical profile of a tutor in a school system. The two tutoring samples included a total of 66 tutoring sessions, each lasting approximately one hour. There were 44 sessions in the research methods corpus and 22 in the mathematics corpus. These 66 tutoring sessions were videotaped, transcribed, and analyzed in detail, both qualitatively and quantitatively.

This chapter will not discuss all the details of the data collection, the scoring of protocols, and the analyses of the tutoring sessions, since this information is available in other published outlets (Graesser & Person, 1994; Graesser, Person, & Magliano, 1995; Person, 1994; Person, Graesser, Magliano, & Kreuz, 1994; Person, Kreuz, Zwaan, & Graesser, 1995). However, we do want to emphasize three critical points.

- First, the topics in the tutoring sessions were very difficult for the students to master. In the mathematics corpus, the teacher deliberately recommended tutoring for students who were having problems with particular topics. In the research methods corpus, the six selected topics—operational definitions of variables, graphing data, inferential statistics, generating an experimental design to test a hypothesis, factorial designs, and interactions between variables—were challenging for virtually all college students.

- Second, the students had already been exposed to the topics prior to the tutoring sessions. All of the students had received at least one lecture on the topic and had been assigned readings in a textbook. In fact, the students in the research methods course were tutored only if they claimed they had read the assigned textbook material.

- Third, the dialogue patterns and pedagogical strategies were quite similar in the two samples of tutoring. In almost all of the analyses that we performed, there were no differences between the 44 research methods sessions and the 22 mathematics tutoring sessions. Therefore, we will not differentiate these two samples when presenting results and making conclusions.

Our dissection of the anatomy of tutoring included both macroanalyses and microanalyses. At the macro level, we analyzed major chunks of student-tutor interaction. For example, we were interested in the examples that were selected, the subtopics that were covered, the major questions that were asked, and the pedagogical strategies that were applied. At the micro level, we performed detailed analyses of the sequences of turns in the tutorial dialogue, the speech acts within each turn, the information quality of contributions, and the feedback that speakers gave to each other's contributions. For example, we analyzed the evolution of conversation when the student and tutor worked on example problems and answered difficult questions. One important microanalysis was a *turn transition matrix.* This analysis traced the evolution of the collaborative exchange by observing the category and quality of contribution $N+1$, given that the student and tutor had together achieved a particular level of quality during contributions 1 through N. Turn transition matrices were prepared for each tutor and student in order to identify particular strategies and conversational styles of individuals.

We are not aware of any other study that has performed a detailed anatomy of a reasonably large corpus of naturalistic tutoring sessions. Previous studies of tutoring processes have had either a very small sample of tutors and tutoring sessions or have used accomplished tutors that applied ideal tutoring strategies (Fox, 1993; Lepper, Aspinwall, Mumme, & Chabay, 1990; McArthur, Stasz, & Zmuidzinas, 1990; Merrill, Reiser, Ranney, & Trafton, 1992; Putnam, 1987). A great deal of time, effort, and funding is needed to perform an in-depth qualitative analysis of tutorial dialogue, so it is not surprising that sample sizes have been small in previous studies. The present project had a large enough sample of tutors and sessions to offer general conclusions about the anatomy of tutoring. With this anatomy in hand, an important direction for future research is to relate the components in this anatomy to student achievement and learning outcomes.

PEDAGOGICAL COMPONENTS THAT RARELY OCCUR IN NATURALISTIC TUTORING

This section identifies some ideal pedogogical components that were conspicuously *absent* in our samples of naturalistic tutoring. These components have been advocated by researchers in education and cognitive science, but they do not naturally emerge during typical tutoring. A tutor will need to be trained on the use of these pedagogical components if they are to be used in tutoring sessions. The components that are conspicuously absent are:

1. active student learning,
2. convergence toward shared meanings (or what some researchers call *student modeling*),
3. error diagnosis,
4. anchored learning, and
5. sophisticated ideal pedagogical strategies.

Given that these components are not prevalent in naturalistic tutoring, they cannot explain the effectiveness of tutoring by normal unskilled tutors.

Active Student Learning

Educational researchers have frequently preached the virtues of students' becoming active self-regulators of their learning instead of passive recipients of information (Brown, 1988; Bruner, 1961; Papert, 1980; Scardamalia & Bereiter, 1991; Wittrock, 1990; Zimmerman, Bandura, & Martinez-Pons, 1992). According to this view, students should be encouraged to ask questions, introduce subtopics, select example problems, and actively rectify their knowledge deficits. In a classroom setting, it would be impractical to have 30 students simultaneously badgering the teacher with questions, subtopics, and examples. Tutoring sessions, however, do provide the opportunity for active student learning.

The tutoring protocols uncovered very little support for active student learning (Graesser et al., 1995). It was the tutor, not the student, who directed the activities in a tutoring session. The tutor established the ground rules and format of all tutoring sessions. None of the students began the session by declaring his or her knowledge deficits and proposing an agenda for the session. The students introduced only 7% of the subtopics and proposed only 4% of the example problems to work on. Most of these student-initiated subtopics and examples were prompted by the tutor (e.g., "Where are you having problems?" or "Which of the problems are difficult for you?"). Only 20% of the questions were asked by the student. This 20% figure is higher than the 4% typically found in a classroom, but the majority of the students' questions during tutoring were attempts to clarify what was said or done in the tutoring session (e.g., "Are you talking about the control condition?") or to verify an existing belief (e.g., "Isn't a nominal scale the same as a categorical scale?"). Only 29% of the student questions, approximately eight per hour, addressed their knowledge deficits (e.g., "When is it okay to use a correlational design?"). Therefore, the available data fail to paint the picture of students being active learners during tutoring sessions.

We are convinced that students need to be *trained* how to be active learners. Students are rarely active, inquisitive self-regulators of learning. These cognitive activities have perhaps been extinguished in classrooms because these settings emphasize the transmission of inert knowledge and cannot accommodate multiple students being inquisitive within a short time span (Bereiter & Scardamalia, 1986; Bransford, Franks, Vye, & Sherwood, 1989; Brown, Bransford, Ferrara, & Campione, 1983; Poole, 1994). Students perhaps need extensive training on the skills of perceiving and rectifying their own knowledge deficits. When students do receive training on question asking and other skills of self-regulatory learning, their learning does improve (King, 1992; Palincsar & Brown, 1984; Pressley, 1995; Pressley, El-Dinary, & Brown, 1992; Pressley, Ghetala, Woloshyn, & Pirie, 1990).

Convergence Toward Shared Meanings

One conceivable advantage of tutoring is an enhanced "meeting of the minds" between the student and tutor. That is, the tutor infers the idiosyncratic knowledge, bugs, and misconceptions of the student, and the student's knowledge base drifts toward the tutor's knowledge base. This convergence toward shared meanings has been proposed by Roschelle (1992) in the context of collaborative learning. Designers of many intelligent tutoring systems have implemented *student modeling*, which is an attempt to infer the knowledge states of a student on the basis of the student's questions, answers to questions, and solutions to problems (Anderson et al., 1995; Ohlsson, 1986). In addition, theories of conversation have frequently emphasized the importance of establishing shared meanings for successful communication (Clark & Schaefer, 1989).

We are convinced, however, that there is a very slow convergence of shared meanings during the course of tutoring. The gap in knowledge between the tutor and student is frighteningly wide and persistent. The forest of student knowledge is so incomplete, vague, imprecise, and littered with misconceptions that it would take too long for the tutor to induce and untangle it, let alone to repair it. On the other side of the coin, the tutor's knowledge is too complex for the student to master during an hour. So the tutor and student continue to operate in substantially different mental spaces. The tutor may believe that whatever is said and done during tutoring is understood by the student, but that is merely an illusion. In actuality, it often bounces off the mind of the student, just as it failed to penetrate the student's knowledge base when the textbook was read or when the lecture was given in the classroom.

We discovered that feedback mechanisms are seriously flawed when tutors and students communicate (Person, 1994; Person et al., 1994). Consider first the feedback that students give on how well they understand the material. Both classroom teachers and tutors frequently ask comprehension-gauging questions (e.g., "Do you understand?", "Are you following?", or "Okay?"). The students respond with positive feedback ("Yes, I understand," a rapid head nod), negative feedback ("No, I don't follow," a facial frown), or indecisive feedback ("I don't know," no answer, a blank stare). Unfortunately, the students' feedback was not a valid reflection of their actual understanding, perhaps because students are very poor at calibrating their comprehension of material (Glenberg, Wilkinson, & Epstein, 1982; Weaver & Bryant, 1995). We found that the correlation was low (.05) between student achievement (i.e., examination scores) and the likelihood of giving positive feedback to the tutor's comprehension-gauging questions. Surprisingly, the correlation was highly positive (.42) between student achievement and the likelihood of giving *negative* feedback. Thus, it was the high-achieving students who claimed they did *not* understand the material (see also Chi, Bassock, Lewis, Reimann, & Glaser, 1989). Overall, student feedback can be misleading in addition to imprecise.

Next consider the feedback that the tutor gives to the student after the student's contributions. After a student contributes information, the tutor often gives immediate short feedback on the quality of the contribution: positive ("Yeah," "Uh-huh," "That's right," "Good," head nod), negative ("No," "Not quite," head shake, facial frown), or neutral ("Okay"). The tutor occasionally gives more lengthy feedback, but most of the feedback comes immediately at the beginning of the tutor's turn. Our analysis revealed that the tutor's feedback was frequently off the mark when the student's contribution was error-ridden (Graesser et al., 1995). The tutor gave positive feedback 32% of the time and negative feedback only 14% of the time after error-ridden contributions by the student. The tutor's feedback was also flawed after the student gave vague or incoherent contributions: 45% and 4% for positive and negative feedback, respectively. Thus, the tutor gave the wrong feedback when the student's contributions manifested misconceptions, bugs, errors, and incoherence. The sanitized positive feedback suggests that tutors are reluctant to say NO. According to Person et al. (1995), tutors are polite conversational partners in the sense that they minimize criticism and other face-threatening acts. The students presumably are less prone to clam up when the tutor maximizes positive feedback and minimizes criticism (Lepper et al., 1990). However, there is a pedagogical trade-off in using this strategy because the accuracy of the tutor's feedback is flawed. If the tutor gives indiscriminate feedback, it is more difficult for the student to acquire accurate knowledge.

There were other analyses that support the claim that tutors and students have a slow convergence on shared meanings. Student achievement was not significantly correlated with the frequency of student questions or the proportion of student questions that reflect knowledge deficits (Person et al., 1994). Although good students did ask a higher proportion of deep-reasoning questions (e.g., *what if, why, how*), the frequency of these questions was so low that it would be difficult for the tutor to use it as a reliable index of student knowledge. Tutors rarely attempted to troubleshoot or to verify the accuracy of student knowledge by asking follow-up questions and giving follow-up example problems. The protocol below illustrates what a good tutor should do, but what tutors rarely do in naturalistic tutoring sessions.

TUTOR: Do you have any problem with these kinds of word problems *(referring to section in book)*, where they say …
STUDENT: *(interrupts)* Uh, not really.

TUTOR: You don't. You don't? You don't have any problem with that?
STUDENT: No.
TUTOR: Let's just do one of them. Um, Dan earned 56 dollars, which is twice more than what Jim earns. Now you're supposed to write an equation.
STUDENT: Uh—I can't write equations.

If it is true that tutors do not deeply understand the mental spaces of students, then it becomes more feasible to simulate normal unskilled tutoring on a computer. One of the main bottlenecks in building intelligent tutoring systems has been natural language understanding. Simply put, it is virtually impossible to program a computer to simulate natural language understanding at deep conceptual levels. However, if effective unskilled tutors have a minimal understanding of student contributions, then we need not expect our computer program to deeply understand the student either.

Error Diagnosis

When a student makes an error, an ideal tutor should acknowledge that the error occurred, identify the error, diagnose the bug or misconception that explains the error, instruct the student how to repair the error, and set new goals that correct the problem. This is the typical approach to handling errors in contemporary intelligent tutoring systems (Anderson et al., 1995; Lesgold et al., 1992; Reiser, Connelly, Ranney, & Ritter, 1992). The downside of this approach is that a poor student might become discouraged when bombarded with a massive dose of negative feedback and criticism. An alternative approach would be to give indirect guidance when students manifest errors, bugs, and misconceptions (Fox, 1993; Lepper, Woolverton, Mumme, & Gunter, in press).

Our unskilled tutors did not devote much effort to diagnosing, dissecting, and troubleshooting student errors (see also McArthur et al., 1990; Putnam, 1987). This is an extremely difficult task for unskilled tutors, skilled tutors, and intelligent tutoring systems alike.

When a student committed an error, the tutor acknowledged that an error occurred 24% of the time, pointed out where the error was 8% of the time, and never explained the bug or misconception that caused the error (Person, 1994). However, student errors were not ignored by the tutor. Later in this chapter we will discuss the various ways that tutors handled student errors. The important point, from the present standpoint, is that real tutors rarely diagnose the *causes* of errors.

Anchored Learning

Educators sometimes attempt to anchor learning material to familiar, real-life situations of students. For example, Bransford and his associates have developed a videodisc technology, called JASPER (Bransford, Goldman, & Vye, 1991; Goldman, Pelligrino, & Bransford, 1993), that presents contextually rich situations and problems that a child might encounter in the real world (e.g., saving an injured animal in the middle of a forest). Groups of children spend several hours solving each of these "authentic" problems. In addition to tapping everyday world knowledge, the solutions lead students to discover important principles that are associated with the learning material. Students actively discover and use the critical knowledge rather than passively receive didactic declarative information.

Our tutors had the opportunity to anchor tutoring topics in authentic learning scenarios, but this approach was virtually nonexistent in the tutoring sessions. Person (1994) analyzed approximately 1000 example problems (i.e., cases) that occurred in the 44 tutoring sessions on research methods. Less than 2% of these examples were elaborated richly enough to be regarded as authentic, *situated examples*. The vast majority of these situated examples were not covered by the tutor and student for a lengthy time period. That is, the tutors never spent 30 minutes collaboratively solving a single example, which is in the spirit of anchored learning. The tutoring sessions did have a large number of example problems, as will be discussed later. However, they were not the authentic, elaborate, situated examples, anchored in real-life situations, that are highly motivating to students.

Sophisticated Pedagogical Strategies

The tutoring protocols were examined for the presence of sophisticated pedagogical strategies that have been proposed by researchers in education and cognitive science (Graesser et al., 1995; Person, 1994).

Specifically, there was a hunt for vestiges of the following strategies: the Socratic method (Stevens, Collins, & Goldin, 1982), modeling-scaffolding-fading (Collins, Brown, & Newman, 1989; Rogoff, 1990), the reciprocal training method (Palincsar & Brown, 1984), building on prerequisites (Gagne, 1977), and the cascade method (VanLehn, Jones, & Chi, 1992). These sophisticated techniques were virtually nonexistent in the tutoring protocols. This result is not particularly surprising, however, because tutors need to be trained for several hours on how to use these exotic techniques; it is unlikely that they would naturally emerge in the unskilled tutor's repertoire. Given the absence of these sophisticated strategies in the tutoring sessions, we do not feel the need to define them in this chapter. However, we will briefly report two analyses to illustrate how the presence of a strategy was assessed.

When the Socratic method is used, the tutor asks a series of carefully crafted questions that lead students to discover their own bugs and misconceptions. When a student produces an error-ridden contribution, the tutor does not explicitly point out the error and correct it; instead, the tutor asks another question and hopes that the student discovers the misconception while answering the question. In this fashion, the student actively discovers the knowledge deficits. Thus, the Socratic method offers a specific prediction: After a student commits an error, the tutor should ask a question designed to elicit an answer that unveils the misconception. However, the tutoring protocols revealed that tutors asked such questions only 3% of the time on the turn that followed an error-ridden student contribution (Person, 1994). This result fails to support the presence of the Socratic method in naturalistic tutoring.

Use of the cascade method requires the tutor to be sensitive to the student's ability to solve example problems. Whenever the student commits errors on example problem N, the tutor should select an easier problem for example N+1. Person (1994) scaled all of the problems in the tutoring corpus on example difficulty in order to test this prediction. She found that 13% of the N+1 examples were easier than example N when students committed errors on example N; 17% of the N+1 examples were more difficult. These results are opposite to the prediction of the cascade method.

Implications of the Missing Pedagogical Components in Naturalistic Tutoring

This section has identified several pedagogical components that are conspicuously absent in naturalistic tutoring with unskilled tutors. These components include active student learning, convergence toward shared meanings, error diagnosis, anchored learning, and sophisticated pedagogical strategies. There are three important implications of these results.

1. These pedagogical components cannot explain the advantage of unskilled tutoring over traditional classroom learning experiences. These components are absent in naturalistic tutoring, so other components must be responsible for the effectiveness of unskilled tutors.
2. Tutors need to be trained how to implement these pedagogical components.
3. The application of these pedagogical components may produce learning gains that exceed the use of unskilled tutors. One direction for future research is to explore this possibility.

PEDAGOGICAL COMPONENTS THAT ARE PREVALENT IN NATURALISTIC TUTORING

What *do* unskilled tutors do during naturalistic tutoring? Four major approaches were identified in naturalistic tutoring:

   (a)   extensive use of examples,

   (b)   curriculum scripts,

   (c)   explanatory reasoning, and

   (d)   collaborative problem solving and question answering.

Some of these are more prevalent in tutoring than in the classroom, so they would be good candidates for explaining the effectiveness of tutoring. Most of these components could be simulated on computer. To the extent that this is possible, a computer simulation of an unskilled tutor might well be within our grasp.

Use of Example Problems

There probably is not a single educator alive who is not convinced of the importance of having students work on example problems. Most intelligent tutoring systems present students with a large number of example problems and use a variety of scaffolding techniques to help the student solve them (Anderson et al., 1995; Lesgold et al., 1992; VanLehn, 1990). According to some empirical studies reported by Sweller (1988), it is better to present a large number of example problems with worked-out solutions than to require students to solve fewer problems on their own. Thus, the process of learning the examples and solutions produces greater learning gains than the process of active discovery of solutions (perhaps because students flounder at these tasks). LeFevre and Dixon (1986) conducted a series of studies on memory for procedural texts that contained both examples and the generic steps in a procedure. The examples had a much greater impact on memory and comprehension than did the generic procedures. Most classroom teachers, however, cover didactic declarative knowledge (such as facts, claims, and principles) to a greater extent than they present and solve example problems. Perhaps naturalistic tutoring is superior to classroom activities because tutoring focuses more on presenting example problems.

The use of example problems was very prevalent in our two samples of naturalistic tutoring. Graesser et al. (1995) reported that

80% of the tutors' questions were asked in the context of an example (67% in the research methods corpus and 92% in the mathematics corpus). In Person's (1994) analysis of the examples in the research methods corpus, the tutors presented an average of 26 examples per hour. The tutor and student interacted extensively on each example: the mean number of conversational turns per example was 19. Thus, even though the examples were not situated in real-life scenarios, there was a large number of examples in the tutoring sessions, and each example occupied a nontrivial amount of the tutoring time.

We recently analyzed the lectures of the instructor in the research methods course in order to calculate the frequency of examples in the lecture. We focused on those lectures that covered the same content as the topics in the tutoring sessions. The instructor incorporated only eight examples per hour in the lecture. Thus, the tutoring sessions introduced approximately three times as many examples as the lectures. There obviously needs to be additional research to obtain more accurate estimates of the rate of examples in tutoring versus classroom settings. However, *the available data do support the conclusion that examples are more prevalent in tutoring than in classroom settings. The density of examples is an excellent candidate for explaining the superiority of naturalistic tutoring.*

It would not be difficult to incorporate examples in a computer simulation of the unskilled tutor. In fact, example generation has already been implemented in four decades of software development in computer-assisted instruction and intelligent tutoring systems. The computer can store a large inventory of example problems.

The examples can be classified according to subtopic, level of difficulty, and the conditions that determine when a particular example should be used. Whenever presenting an example, the computer-tutor would precede it with a question or request (e.g., "How would you solve the following problem?" or "Try solving the following problem"). The obvious challenge is to determine how the computer can direct the tutorial dialogue while the student solves the problem. That challenge is addressed later in this chapter.

Curriculum Scripts

A curriculum script provides a top-down organization of the subtopics covered in a classroom or tutoring session. The content of each subtopic includes a didactic elaboration of the subtopic, a set of examples, and a set of questions. There may be a rigid ordering of the subtopics and the content within each subtopic; however, there normally is some flexibility in this ordering. Skilled tutors are known to use curriculum scripts (McArthur et al., 1990; Putnam, 1987). We examined our protocols to assess whether unskilled tutors do so as well.

The unskilled tutors did indeed make heavy use of curriculum scripts. A tutor tended to introduce the same subtopics, present the same examples, and ask the same questions for several students who were tutored on the same topic. Person (1994) analyzed the source and consistency of the tutors' examples in order to assess the prevalence of curriculum scripts. She found that 27% of the examples were taken directly from the textbook, and another 51% of the examples were presented to two or more of the students. Only 17% of the examples were spontaneously generated by the tutor and presented to only one student, presumably in an effort to handle the idiosyncratic constraints of the local context and the knowledge of the student. Therefore, according to Person's analyses, 78% of the tutors' examples were furnished by curriculum scripts in a top-down fashion.

Although curriculum scripts were very prevalent in the tutoring sessions, this component is not unique to tutoring. Curriculum scripts provide the backbone of classroom planning and instruction. Therefore, we do not believe that curriculum scripts are responsible for the advantages of the unskilled tutor over the classroom teacher.

Once again, it should not be difficult to simulate curriculum scripts on a computer. Curriculum scripts have already been implemented in hundreds of computer programs in the arena of computer-assisted instruction and intelligent tutoring. The lessons, examples, and questions are mechanically presented by the computer in a top-down fashion. The challenge lies elsewhere, such as in the problems of interpreting the contributions of the student and formulating responses to those contributions.

Explanatory Reasoning

Explanatory reasoning is an important manifestation of deep understanding of material. Explanatory reasoning delineates the causes and consequences of events, the reasons for performing actions, the justifications for decisions, and the logical foundations of claims. The important question types that elicit explanatory reasoning are *why*, *why-not*, *how*, *what-if*, *what-if-not*, and *what-are-the-consequences* (Graesser & Person, 1994). Explanations that follow from these questions tie together the content of the material by providing functional, causal, or logical structures. Therefore, explanations both elaborate and impose coherence on the material to be learned.

There is ample evidence that explanations improve comprehension and memory for material. Memory for unrelated facts is facilitated when subjects are instructed to explain why the facts exist (Pressley, Symons, McDaniel, Snyder, & Turner, 1988). Memory and comprehension for stories is positively correlated with the extent to which readers generate explanations for the story events (Graesser, Singer, & Trabasso, 1994; Trabasso & Suh, 1993). There is a similar correlation for scientific text (Chi, de Leeuw, Chiu, & LaVancher, 1994). There are some additional facts about explanations that are particularly intriguing. First, explanations are particularly effective in promoting learning when the students themselves—as opposed to the teacher, experimenter, or text—generate the explanations (Pressley, Wood, Woloshyn, Martin, King, & Menk, 1992; Webb, 1989). Second, an explanation that is merely presented to a student may have little or no impact on learning gains, but gains are realized when a student uses it as an explanation to another student (Webb, Troper, & Fall, 1995). Third, the students' self-explanations need not be objectively accurate for them to improve comprehension and memory (Chi et al., 1989; Chi et al., 1994). Flawed self-explanations may be sufficient to achieve coherent memory representations and reasoning that is approximately accurate. Therefore, tutors should be encouraged to prompt students to construct self-explanations of facts and events in the learning material (Lepper et al., 1990) and to actively articulate the explanations that are supplied by the tutor.

Explanatory reasoning was very prevalent in the naturalistic tutoring sessions. The frequency of deep-reasoning questions (*why*, *how*, *what-if*, etc.) was computed in the research methods corpus and mathematics corpus (Graesser & Person, 1994; Graesser et al., 1995). The unskilled tutors asked 19 deep-reasoning questions per hour. This rate is quite high compared to the rate in a classroom, which averages about 5 per hour (Dillon, 1988; Kerry, 1987). Thus, *deep-reasoning questions are about 4 times as plentiful in tutoring sessions as in classroom instruction*. Teachers perhaps do not have the time to ask many deep-reasoning questions in a classroom. It takes a long time to answer these questions, and it is difficult to understand the lengthy answers. Consequently, teachers settle for easy, shallow, short-answer questions that grill the students on explicit material.

Explanatory reasoning was also manifested in the student questions. An average student asked eight deep-reasoning questions per hour in the tutoring sessions (Graesser & Person, 1994). In contrast, student questions are quite rare in classrooms, according to dozens of published studies (Dillon, 1988). The reported incidence of student questions in a classroom is 0.1 questions per student per hour. The rate of student questions in the classroom lectures on research methods was 0.2 questions per student per hour. Thus, students clearly asked more deep-reasoning questions in tutoring sessions than in the classroom, even though questions were not extremely frequent during tutoring. It is also interesting to note that higher-achieving students in the research methods corpus asked a higher proportion of deep-reasoning questions than students with lower grades and examination scores.

In summary, we are convinced that explanatory reasoning is more prevalent in naturalistic tutoring than in classroom settings. This pedagogical component is another good candidate for explaining the advantages of tutoring over the classroom.

Is it possible for a computer to simulate the explanatory reasoning that is exhibited in naturalistic tutoring? Some aspects of explanatory reasoning may be possible to imitate. The curriculum script would include a set of deep-reasoning questions that the computer-tutor asks about the various subtopics. The student would then type in answers to the computer's questions. What is so intriguing is that *the computer does not need to deeply interpret the students' self-explanations.* In fact, the tutor might not need to interpret the student's explanations at all! As we discussed earlier, the unskilled tutor does not comprehend the student's contributions at much, if any, depth, so we would not expect the computer to do this either. The activity of constructing self-explanations does facilitate the student's comprehension and memory, but these self-explanations need not be dissected, diagnosed, and debugged by the tutor. Unskilled tutors do not do this, so the computer need not do it either.

Nevertheless, there are two instances when the computer-tutor would be challenged in implementing explanatory reasoning. The first is when the student asks a deep-reasoning question. How would the computer formulate an answer? Unfortunately, the ability of computers to comprehend language and discourse is quite limited. There has been some progress in getting a computer to interpret student questions and generate explanations in tutorial dialogue (Cawsey, 1993; Moore, 1994; Paris, 1993), but the success of these systems is not even close to passing the Turing test (i.e., such that students cannot accurately decide whether they are communicating with a computer or another person).

The second instance is when the student needs help in answering the tutor's deep-reasoning questions. As will be discussed in the next section, students rarely produce a complete answer when a tutor asks a deep-reasoning question. Instead, there is a collaborative dialogue between student and tutor that involves several conversational turns. So the computer will need to apply scaffolding techniques to help the student answer the question. These collaborative scaffolding techniques are discussed in the next section.

Collaborative Question Answering and Problem Solving

One of the key components that sets tutoring apart from classroom settings is the collaborative dialogue between tutor and student. It is impossible for the teacher to have simultaneous dialogues with 30 different students in a classroom, whereas one-to-one dialogue is perhaps the most salient feature of tutoring. Collaboration among peers has been one of the popular contemporary trends in education (Bransford et al., 1991; Brown, 1992, 1994; King, 1994; Madden, Slavin, Karweit, Dolan, & Wasik, 1993; Rogoff, 1990; Schwartz, 1995; Slavin, 1983). More empirical research is needed to assess the extent to which collaboration *per se* is responsible for learning gains. However, if collaboration is an important pedagogical component, then it may be partly responsible for the effectiveness of tutoring.

Patterns of collaboration were analyzed in detail in the research methods and mathematics tutoring corpora. The primary focus was on the collaboration patterns that exist in the context of example problems and the deep-reasoning questions asked by tutors. We concentrated our attention on these contexts because examples and deep reasoning are the two most likely components to explain the effectiveness of tutoring. It is important to emphasize that collaboration was extensive in these two contexts. When the tutor and student solved an example problem, the mean number of conversational turns was 19 (Person, 1994). When the tutor asked a deep-reasoning question, there were approximately 10 conversational turns and the tutor ended up supplying more answer information than the student (Graesser et al., 1995). Thus, it is not the case that the student quickly formulates an answer when the tutor presents an example problem or asks a question. (If that were the case, there would be only one conversational turn—the solution or answer of the student). Instead, there is extensive collaboration and exchange, distributed across several conversational turns.

Five-step Question-Answering Frame. In a typical classroom setting, the teacher grills the students with a large number of questions. The teacher expects a quick answer (Duell, 1994) and calls on another student if the first student fails to supply an answer within one or two seconds. The teacher immediately evaluates the quality of a student response with positive or negative feedback. This is known as the Question-Answer-Evaluation (QAE) sequence, or more generally, the Initiate-Response-Evaluation (IRE) sequence (Mehan, 1979; Sinclair & Coulthart, 1975). There is a large density of QAE sequences in most classrooms; the teacher often launches the questions in quick succession and expects short, snappy answers.

In a typical tutoring session, however, the tutor's questions tend to be deeper and student answers lengthier. Moreover, the tutor augments the QAE (or IRE) sequence by encouraging a collaborative elaboration of the answer. The 3-step QAE sequence is expanded into a 5-step question-answering frame (Graesser & Person, 1994; Graesser et al., 1995), as specified below.

Step 1: Tutor asks question.
Step 2: Student answers question.
Step 3: Tutor gives short evaluation on the quality of the student's answer.
Step 4: Tutor and student collaboratively improve the quality of the answer.
Step 5: Tutor assesses the student's understanding of the answer.

A succinct example of this 5-step question-answering frame follows:

1   TUTOR: Now what is a factorial design?
2   STUDENT: It has two variables.
3   TUTOR: Uh-huh ...
4   TUTOR: So there are two or more independent variables and one ...
        (pause)
    STUDENT: Dependent variable.
5   TUTOR: Do you see that?

In most cases, the collaboration in step 4 is much more extensive than in this example, and actually accounts for most of the conversational turns when a question is answered. Some of the ways that collaboration is achieved are discussed below. In step 5, tutors tend to ask comprehension-gauging questions to assess the students' understanding, as in the example. However, because tutors rarely troubleshoot the students' understanding by asking follow-up questions and giving follow-up example problems, and because students do not accurately calibrate their own comprehension, there is little utility in asking the comprehension-gauging questions. Therefore, we believe that *step 4 is the critical part of the 5-step frame that might explain the advantages of tutoring over classroom activities.*

Pumping. Tutors periodically pump the student for more information during collaborative question answering and problem solving. The pumping occurs primarily in steps 3 and 4 of the question-answering frame. The pumps sometimes consist of positive feedback ("Right," "Yeah," dramatic head nod), but more frequently they consist of neutral feedback ("Uh-huh," "Mmm-hmm," "Okay," subtle head nod) or explicit requests for more information ("Tell me more," "What else?"). Pumping clearly puts the onus on the student to deliver information.

The pumping of the tutor actually serves several conversational functions. First, it provides feedback that acknowledges that the tutor is hearing and understanding what the student is saying. This feedback occurs in normal conversation after every 13 syllables, on average (Clark & Schaefer, 1989). Second, it sometimes provides positive or neutral feedback to a student's contribution. Third, it encourages student contributions by giving the student the "floor" in the conversation (i.e., the student is invited and expected to speak). The following example illustrates the extensive use of pumping in an exchange.

1   TUTOR: Why would a researcher even want to use more than two levels of an independent variable in an experiment?
2   STUDENT: More than two levels?

3   TUTOR: Mmm-hmm.
4   STUDENT: They would, um, it'd be real accurate 'cause it would show if
         there's a curvilinear.
5   TUTOR: Mmm-hmm.
6   STUDENT: Uh, let's see ... um, they, like, show partial effects and, um,
         correlational effects?
7   TUTOR: Mmm-hmm.
8   STUDENT: I think ...
9   TUTOR: Yeah. Okay. And what's meant by a factorial design?

The tutor's pump at turn 5 occurs after a correct student contribution. However, the student's answer is not complete, so the tutor
pumps for more information. The tutor's pump at turn 7 occurs after
an error-ridden student contribution. As discussed earlier, the tutor
does not give negative feedback and does not correct the error, but
instead pumps the student for more information with neutral feedback. At turn 9, the tutor gives positive feedback in spite of the fact
that a completely correct answer never emerged. The *Mmm-hmm*
response at turn 3 is interesting. It serves as both an answer to the
student's counter-clarification question and a neutral pump for
information. So there are three *Mmm-hmm*'s, but the functions of
each *Mmm-hmm* are somewhat different (see Fox, 1993; Smith &
Clark, 1993).

   It might be feasible to implement the pumping mechanism in a
computer simulation of the unskilled tutor. The primary goal of this
pumping mechanism would be to encourage the student to articulate
self-explanations and solutions to problems, not to give corrective
feedback. The computer would respond "Uh-huh," "What else?", or
"Tell me more" after the computer asks the question (or presents an
example problem) and the student gives the first contribution.
Human tutors normally pump the student for one cycle after the
student gives the first contribution, regardless of the quality of the
contribution. The computer would present additional pumps later in
the evolution of the answer (or solution to an example problem). It
would not need to comprehend the student's contribution at a deep

level or supply negative feedback to error-ridden contributions, as discussed earlier. It could altogether avoid comprehending the student's contribution at any level, and simply respond "Uh-huh" or "Okay" after the student's contributions. Alternatively, it might perform a shallow semantic analysis (Dahlgren, 1988) of the student's contributions and give negative feedback when there are contradictions between true domain knowledge and what the student says.

Unskilled tutors do give negative feedback to simple false propositions (e.g., *4 times 7 is 21* or *shoe size is measured on a nominal scale*), but they rarely give negative feedback to lengthy explanations and questions that do not have clear-cut, well-defined answers (Person et al., 1995). The most successful computer systems that simulate natural language comprehension can handle shallow semantics to a limited extent, but cannot achieve deep comprehension. The computer would give negative feedback to the extent that it is capable of interpreting the student's contributions and the extent to which it detects false or contradictory student claims.

Prompting. Tutors sometimes prompt students with a rich discourse context and expect them to fill in a missing word or phrase. A pause or intonation cue signifies that the student is expected to fill in this information. For example, the tutor might say, "As you know by now, correlation does not mean … *(pause),*" and expect the student to fill in "causation." In normal everyday conversation, a cooperative listener is expected to help the speaker speak by filling in words and by repairing speech errors (Clark & Schaefer, 1989). Unskilled tutors capitalize on this feature of conversation by intentionally prompting the student to fill in information. This encourages the student to be more actively involved in the dialogue.

The computer could simulate the prompting of an unskilled tutor by implementing a cloze technique. As the computer prints out messages, it would periodically leave out the final word and insert an underline cue; the cue signifies that the student is supposed to fill in the missing information. For example, the computer would print out the following message: "As you know by now, correlation does not mean _____." Of course, there would be a judicious selection of the words and phrases the student is supposed to fill in. After the student fills in the information, the computer could print out the correct word or phrase and thereby give the student indirect feedback about the quality of his or her answers. In fact, unskilled tutors often provide this corrective feedback when the information is short and clear-cut.

Splicing. Splicing is the technique unskilled tutors used most frequently when students produced error-ridden or incoherent contributions. When the tutor detects an error, he or she jumps in and splices in a correct answer (Graesser et al., 1995; Person, 1994). This splicing is also a frequent activity in normal conversations (Ferrara, 1992). Sometimes the splicing is so quick that the tutor interrupts the student, as in the following example.

> TUTOR: According to the graph, how should memory be affected by imagery?
> STUDENT: It should get worse because ...
> TUTOR: *(interrupts)* It should get *better* because ...

At other times, however, the splicing occurs at the tutor's next conversational turn, as illustrated below.

> TUTOR: If you're doing a line graph and you have group A and group B, how would you make a line graph?
> STUDENT: You'd plot the individual scores on the X axis and the Y axis and you'd connect them. [**This is an error-ridden answer.**]
> TUTOR: So if you are showing the relationship between A and B, would it be correct to put a point at each group's mean and put a line on it? [**This second clause includes the splice**]
> STUDENT: Yeah.

As mentioned above, splicing was the technique unskilled tutors used most frequently in handling students' errors. Splicing occurred after 38% of the students' error-ridden contributions in the answers to deep-reasoning questions, and after 31% of the errors during joint problem solving (Person, 1994). The likelihood that a tutor gave a partially correct or completely correct answer to a question on contribution N+1 varied systematically as a function of the quality of the student's contribution N (Graesser et al., 1995): 0.59, 0.62, 0.58, and 0.81 for the quality states of N being completely correct, partially correct, vague, and error-ridden, respectively. In a reanalysis of the data, we found the following percentages for completely correct answers of the tutor: 0.16, 0.11, 0.08, and 0.20 after student contributions that were completely correct, partially correct, vague, and error-ridden, respectively. The comparatively high values associated with error-ridden contributions support the claim that tutors splice in correct and complete answers when they hear erroneous output from the student. Perhaps the tutor does not want to hear the errors. Alternatively, perhaps the tutor believes that correct information might obliterate the errors in the student's knowledge base.

It would be tricky to implement splicing in a computer simulation of the unskilled tutor. The computer would need to have some ability to comprehend the students' contributions. This could range from shallow semantics to a deep global comprehension. In any case, simulating splicing would require interpretation of the student's contributions, detection of errors, and generation of the appropriate correct responses. Given that computer models of comprehension are quite limited, it might be prudent to eliminate splicing altogether in the computer simulation. Without that ability, the computer would be simulating a shallow unskilled tutor.

Hinting. Unskilled tutors occasionally give hints when students fail to give any contributions or give error-ridden contributions. The tutor presents a fact, asks a leading question, or reframes the problem. Some classes of hints given by ideal tutors and intelligent tutoring systems are quite sophisticated (Hume, Michael, Rovick, & Evens, 1996; McArthur et al., 1990; Merrill et al., 1992), but the hints of the unskilled tutor are not particularly sophisticated.

Consider first the hints that unskilled tutors give when students either fail to give an answer to a question or give a vague answer to the question. The tutor does not chime in with a completely correct answer. Instead, he or she delivers a partially correct answer which presumably cues the student to provide more information. In our analysis of the research methods and mathematics samples, we found that 51% of the tutors' contributions on turn N+1 were partially correct, and 8% were completely correct, after the student gave no answer or a vague answer on turn N. In fact, as reported above, completely correct tutor answers were least likely to occur after a student gave no answer or a vague answer; they were more likely to follow completely correct, partially correct, or error-ridden student answers. Hints comprise a subset of the tutor's partially correct answers. In most cases the tutor revises the question or elaborates the context to prompt a correct response from the student. The example below illustrates how hinting can be combined with prompting to elicit the correct answer from a student.

TUTOR: What type of scale would that be?
STUDENT: Oh, let me think, which one. I don't know.
TUTOR: Try to think. Nominal or ... *(pause)* ?
STUDENT: Ordinal, yeah.
TUTOR: It would be. Why would it be an ordinal scale?

Most hints are fairly direct and lead the student to produce a fairly specific answer, as in this example. However, occasionally hints are more remote and require more thought by the student.

Consider next the hints that occur after error-ridden student contributions. In our analysis, we found that tutor hints followed 27% of the students' error-ridden contributions in deep-reasoning contexts and 11% of error-ridden contributions in example contexts. Most of the hints were direct and designed to elicit a particular response from the student, but some hints were more remote and thought-provoking. The example below illustrates how hinting can be combined with splicing in an effort to elicit a particular answer from the student.

> TUTOR: Okay. Is there anything else about this graph that you would want to do before you finish? I mean, do you consider this finished?
>
> STUDENT: I guess I could, I could draw a line.
>
> TUTOR: *(interrupting)* What if you walked up to this graph and you had never seen it?
>
> STUDENT: Oh, I guess I should label these *(points to the axes).*
>
> TUTOR: Yeah, yeah.

The tutor spliced in a question as soon as she realized that the student was on the wrong track at the second turn. Thus, splicing was combined with hinting.

A perfect computer simulation of unskilled hinting would presumably be impossible to achieve without a deep comprehension of the student's contributions. After all, a good hint has to be delivered at the right time in the evolution of the student contributions. However, we did not analyze the effectiveness and appropriateness of the hints that the unskilled tutors gave to the students. Additional research needs to be conducted to explore hinting in naturalistic tutoring. It is conceivable that most of the hints do not reflect a deep comprehension of the students' contributions. The hints may be canned and preformulated in a fashion that anticipates the problems that the students are likely to have. If this is the case, then the computer simulation could merely contain a set of preformulated hints and give them somewhat indiscriminately after a student enters a minimal or error-ridden contribution. The list of context-sensitive hints would be included as part of the curriculum script. Whenever the hints were not optimally tuned to the context, they would not fit into a natural flow of the dialogue, but they might be perceived as reasonable follow-up questions relevant to the question or example problem. Clearly, however, hinting would be a challenge to the designer of a computer simulation of an unskilled tutor.

Summarizing. A summary of the answer or the example solution is sometimes given at the end of an exchange. These summaries furnish a concise, coherent organization of the answer or solution. This presumably is helpful, considering that the answer or solution evolved over several conversational turns. Graesser et al. (1995) reported that it is the tutor rather than the student who provides these summaries. Tutors had a higher likelihood than students—0.16 versus 0.04—of summarizing the completely correct answer after a complete answer had already emerged in the exchange. Although an accomplished tutor might place the onus on the student to give the summary, this is not what unskilled tutors do.

It would not be a challenge to implement tutor summaries in a computer simulation of an unskilled tutor. A canned correct summary would be associated with each question and example problem in the curriculum script. This summary would be given after the computer determined that the tutor and student had played out the dialogue in the context of a question or example problem. The placement of the summary may not matter that much, as long as it appears towards the end of the exchange. A simple rule would be to give the summary after a fixed number of conversational turns. Alternatively, it could be contingent on the quality of the information in the exchange, but that would require the computer to interpret the student contributions.

CONCLUSIONS

This chapter has dissected the anatomy of naturalistic tutoring with unskilled tutors. After analyzing the tutoring protocols of college students being tutored in research methods and seventh graders being tutored in mathematics, we identified the pedagogical components that are prevalent in naturalistic tutoring and that set it apart from classroom settings. We identified those components that are likely to explain the well-documented advantages of tutoring over classrooms. Finally, we speculated on how feasible it would be to build a computer simulation of the unskilled tutor.

So what is it about tutoring that might be responsible for its superiority over the classroom with respect to learning gains? According to our analyses, the key candidates are the *high density of example problems*, the *comparative emphasis on explanatory reasoning*, and *collaborative question answering and problem solving*. Curriculum scripts are also very prevalent in tutoring, but this component is perhaps more prevalent in classroom settings. The following components are conspicuously absent in tutoring: active student learning, convergence toward shared meanings, discriminating feedback on errors, anchored learning, and sophisticated pedagogical strategies. Therefore, the latter components cannot explain the advantages of naturalistic tutoring.

Is it possible to simulate the unskilled tutor on a computer? This goal would be impossible if the computer had to deeply comprehend the meaning of students' contributions. However, unskilled tutors do *not* achieve a deep comprehension of the students' knowledge base and misconceptions. Therefore, this component may not be essential. We described how a computerized unskilled tutor might simulate the delivery of example problems, curriculum scripts, explanatory reasoning, and some of the features of collaborative question answering and problem solving, such as pumping, prompting, and summarizing. However, it would be much more challenging to simulate answers to student questions and to implement splicing and hinting. These latter challenges will be met to the extent that computers are able to comprehend language and discourse at deeper conceptual levels. Thus, simulation of a shallow unskilled tutor is well within our grasp, but simulation of a full-fledged unskilled tutor is not. But who knows? Perhaps a computerized, shallow, unskilled tutor could end up being quite effective in promoting learning gains—especially in light of its accessibility, as it could be readily available on a nearby computer.

Does our analysis of normal tutoring suggest any strategies that might be used by teachers in classroom settings? We do believe that there is some wisdom that can be transported from tutoring contexts to the classroom. Some of this wisdom reflects what normal unskilled tutors do when they attempt to assist individual learners. Some of the wisdom reflects what we know that tutors do *not* normally do. In both cases, there are some suggestions on how teachers might improve the conversation patterns in classrooms.

1. *Take student questions seriously.* Student questions are infrequent in both classroom and tutoring contexts, so teachers need to take active steps to make the experience more positive and illuminating for the student. Both tutors and teachers have the tendency to dismiss or gloss over student questions in an effort to advance the curriculum script. Positive reinforcement is an obvious way of increasing student question asking (e.g., "Good question!"). Another way is for the teacher to make sure he or she understands the student's question. This can be difficult when there is little shared knowledge between teacher and student. The teacher may need to ask counter-clarification questions to make sure he or she truly understands what the student is asking. If the question is imperfectly understood, the teacher's answer will be inadequate, and student question asking will not prove worthwhile.

2. *Use conversation moves to encourage student contributions.* Pumps and prompts can be used in the classroom, just as in tutoring, to stimulate student contributions in collaborative exchanges. The teacher should expect longer and more frequent contributions from students who have more knowledge. When a student is supplying quality answers to questions or solutions to problems, the teacher should resist the natural temptation to fill in information that the student could supply. Whereas it was the tutors who tended to give summaries of answers to questions and solutions to problems, we recommend that teachers encourage students to give the summaries.

3. *Give discriminating, but polite, feedback to students' error-*

ridden contributions. Tutors tended to give misleading feedback to students after the students produced error-ridden or vague contributions; the feedback was positive more often than negative. Stated differently, real tutors don't say NO. Just as in tutoring, when handling low-quality student contributions, the teacher needs to be sensitive to two different constraints, which sometimes conflict. The feedback needs to be accurate, but it also needs to be polite and encouraging. The teacher should neither gloss over the errors nor discourage the student with a hefty dose of negative feedback. Correct feedback is provided by splicing in correct information immediately after student errors. Polite feedback is provided by hints and follow-up questions that indirectly steer the student back on course. A good teaching style effectively juggles the goals of accuracy, politeness, and the enhancement of student self-esteem.

4. *Never trust students' answers to comprehension-gauging questions ("Do you understand?").* Teachers frequently ask these questions and believe the students when they give positive responses. Unfortunately, most students have no idea how well they understand the material, so the answers are misleading. In fact, it is consistently the better students who say that they do *not* understand. Teachers should not depend on simple comprehension-gauging questions when they assess student understanding. Instead, they should ask follow-up questions and present follow-up problems that reveal the actual level of student understanding.

5. *Ask deep-reasoning questions (e.g., why, how, what-if, what-if-not).* Teachers should resist the temptation to ask shallow questions that address explicit material, have short answers, and involve simple facts or claims. Instead, they should ask questions that invite lengthier answers and tap deep explanatory reasoning. Students rarely whip out a quick and complete answer when deep-reasoning questions are asked, so the teacher needs to be patient and collaborate with the student

while the answers are produced. Collaboration is provided by pumping, prompting, splicing, hinting, and summarizing.

6. *Plan complex material and special teaching strategies in advance.* Complex curricula and pedagogical strategies cannot be manufactured spontaneously in classroom talk, so they must be planned in advance. Example problems, penetrating questions, and the content of the curriculum scripts need to be mapped out by the teacher prior to a class. Sophisticated pedagogical strategies (such as the Socratic method, modeling-scaffolding-fading, the reciprocal training method) do not naturally emerge in tutoring and the classroom. Rather, teachers need to be trained extensively on the use of these strategies.

REFERENCES

Anderson, J.R., Corbett, A.T., Koedinger, K.R., & Pelletier, R. (1995). Cognitive tutors: Lessons learned. *The Journal of the Learning Sciences, 4,* 167-207.

Bereiter, C., & Scardamalia, M. (1986). Educational relevance of the study of expertise. *Interchange, 17,* 10-19.

Bloom, B.S. (1984). The 2-sigma problem: The search for methods of group instruction as effective as one-to-one tutoring. *Educational Researcher, 13,* 4-16.

Bransford, J.D., Franks, J.J., Vye, N.J., & Sherwood, R.D. (1989). New approaches to instruction. In S. Vosniadou & A. Ortony (Eds.), *Similarity and analogical reasoning.* New York: Cambridge University Press.

Bransford, J.D., Goldman, S.R., & Vye, N.J. (1991). Making a difference in people's ability to think: Reflections on a decade of work and some hopes for the future. In R. J. Sternberg & L. Okagaki (Eds.), *Influences on children* (pp. 147-180). Hillsdale, NJ: Erlbaum.

Brown, A.L. (1988). Motivation to learn and understand: On taking charge of one's own learning. *Cognition and Instruction, 5,* 311-321.

Brown, A.L. (1992). Designing experiments: Theoretical and methodological challenges in creating complex interventions in classroom settings. *The Journal of the Learning Sciences, 2,* 141-178.

Brown, A.L. (1994). The advancement of learning. *Educational Researcher, 23*(8), 4-12.

Brown, A.L., Bransford, J.D., Ferrara, R.A., & Campione, J.C. (1983). Learning, remembering, and understanding. In J.H. Flavell & E.M. Markman (Eds.), *Handbook of child psychology* (4th ed.), *Cognitive development, Vol. 3.* New York: John Wiley.

Bruner, J.S. (1961). The act of discovery. *Harvard Educational Review, 31,* 21-32.

Cawsey, A. (1993). *Explanation and interaction: The computer generation of explanatory dialogues.* Cambridge, MA: MIT Press.

Chi, M.T., Bassok, M., Lewis, M.W., Reimann, P., & Glaser, R. (1989). Self-explanations: How students study and use examples in learning to solve problems. *Cognitive Science, 13,* 145-182.

Chi, M.T.H., de Leeuw, N., Chiu, M., & LaVancher, C. (1994). Eliciting self-explanations improves understanding. *Cognitive Science, 18,* 439-477.

Clark, H.H., & Schaefer, E.F. (1989). Contributing to discourse. *Cognitive Science, 13,* 259-294.

Cohen, P.A., Kulik, J.A., & Kulik, C.C. (1982). Educational outcomes of tutoring: A meta-analysis of findings. *American Educational Research Journal, 19,* 237-248.

Collins, A., Brown, J.S., & Newman, S.E. (1989). Cognitive apprenticeship: Teaching the craft of reading, writing, and mathematics. In L.B. Resnick (Ed.), *Knowing, learning, and instruction: Essays in honor of Robert Glaser* (pp. 453-494). Hillsdale, NJ: Erlbaum.

Dahlgren, K. (1988). *Naive semantics for natural language understanding.* Boston: Kluwer Academic Press.

Dillon, J.T. (1988). *Questioning and teaching: A manual of practice.* New York: Teachers College Press.

Duell, O.K. (1994). Extended wait time and university student achievement. *American Educational Research Journal, 31,* 397-414.

Ferrara, K. (1992). The interactive achievement of a sentence: Joint productions in therapeutic discourse. *Discourse Processes, 15,* 207-228.

Fitz-Gibbon, C.R. (1977). *An analysis of the literature of cross-age tutoring.* Washington, DC: National Institute of Education. (ERIC Document Reproduction Service No. ED 148 807).

Fox, B. (1993). *The human tutoring dialogue project.* Hillsdale, NJ: Erlbaum.

Gagne, R.M. (1977). *The conditions of learning* (3rd ed.). New York: Holt, Rinehart, & Winston.

Glenberg, A.M., Wilkinson, A.C., & Epstein, W. (1982). The illusion of knowing: Failure in the assessment of comprehension. *Memory and Cognition, 10,* 597-602.

Goldman, S.R., Pellegrino, J.W., & Bransford, J.D. (1993). Assessing programs that invite thinking. In H. O'Neill & E. Baker (Eds.), *Technology assessment:*

Estimating the future. Hillsdale, NJ: Erlbaum.

Graesser, A.C., & Person, N.K. (1994). Question asking during tutoring. *American Educational Research Journal, 31,* 104-137.

Graesser, A.C., Person, N.K., & Magliano, J.P. (1995). Collaborative dialogue patterns in naturalistic one-to-one tutoring. *Applied Cognitive Psychology, 9,* 359-387.

Graesser, A.C., Singer, M., & Trabasso, T. (1994). Constructing inferences during narrative text comprehension. *Psychological Review, 101,* 371-395.

Hume, G.D., Evens, M.W., Rovick, A., & Michael, J.A. (1996). Hinting as a tactic in one-on-one. *The Journal of Learning Sciences, 5,* 23-47.

Kerry, T. (1987). Classroom questions in England. *Questioning Exchange, 1*(1), 32-33.

King, A. (1992). Comparison of self-questioning, summarizing, and notetaking-review as strategies for learning from lectures. *American Educational Research Journal, 29,* 303-323.

King, A. (1994). Guiding knowledge construction in the classroom: Effects of teaching children how to question and how to explain. *American Educational Research Journal, 31,* 338-368.

LeFevre, J.A., & Dixon, P. (1986). Do written instructions need examples? *Cognition and Instruction, 3,* 1-30.

Lepper, M.R., Aspinwall, L.G., Mumme, D.L., & Chabay, R.W. (1990). Self-perception and social-perception processes in tutoring: Subtle social control strategies of expert tutors. In J.M. Olson & M.P. Zanna (Eds.), *Self-inference processes: The Ontario symposium* (pp. 217-237). Hillsdale, NJ: Erlbaum.

Lepper, M.R., Woolverton, M., Mumme, D.L., & Gunter, J.L. (in press). Motivational techniques of expert human tutors: Lessons for the design of computer-based tutors. In S.P. Lajoie & S. Derry (Eds.), *Computers as cognitive tools.* Hillsdale, NJ: Erlbaum.

Lesgold, A., Lajoie, S., Bunzo, M., & Eggan, G. (1992). SHERLOCK: A coached practice environment for an electronics troubleshooting job. In J.H. Larkin & R.W. Chabay (Eds.), *Computer-assisted instruction and intelligent tutoring systems* (pp. 201-238). Hillsdale, NJ: Erlbaum.

Madden, N., Slavin, R., Karweit, N., Dolan, L., & Wasik, B. (1993). Success for all: Longitudinal effects of a restructuring program for inner-city elementary schools. *American Educational Research Journal, 30,* 123-148.

McArthur, D., Stasz, C., & Zmuidzinas, M. (1990). Tutoring techniques in algebra. *Cognition and Instruction, 7,* 197-244.

Mehan, H. (1979). *Learning lessons: Social organization in the classroom.* Cambridge, MA: Harvard University Press.

Merrill, D.C., Reiser, B.J., Ranney, M., & Trafton, J.G. (1992). Effective tutoring techniques: A comparison of human tutors and intelligent tutoring systems. *The Journal of the Learning Sciences, 2,* 277-305.

Mohan, M. (1972). *Peer tutoring as a technique for teaching the unmotivated.* Fredonia, NY: State University of New York, Teacher Education Research Center. (ERIC Document Reproduction Service No. ED 061 154).

Moore, J.D. (1994). *Participating in explanatory dialogues: Interpreting and responding to questions in context.* Cambridge, MA: MIT Press.

Ohlsson, S. (1986). Some principles of intelligent tutoring. *Instructional Science, 14,* 293-326.

Palincsar, A.S., & Brown, A. (1984). Reciprocal teaching of comprehension-fostering and comprehension-monitoring activities. *Cognition and Instruction, 1,* 117-175.

Papert, S. (1980). *Mindstorms: Children, computers and powerful ideas.* New York: Basic Books.

Paris, C.L. (1993). *User modeling in text generation.* London: Pinter Publishers.

Person, N.K. (1994). *An analysis of the examples that tutors generate during naturalistic one-to-one tutoring sessions.* Unpublished doctoral dissertation, Memphis State University, Memphis, TN.

Person, N.K., Graesser, A.C., Magliano, J.P., & Kreuz, R.J. (1994). Inferring what the student knows in one-to-one tutoring: The role of student questions and answers. *Learning and Individual Differences, 6,* 205-229.

Person, N.K., Kreuz, R.J., Zwaan, R., & Graesser, A.C. (1995). Pragmatics and pedagogy: Conversational rules and politeness strategies may inhibit effective tutoring. *Cognition and Instruction, 13,* 161-188.

Poole, D. (1994). Routine testing practices and the linguistic construction of knowledge. *Cognition and Instruction, 12,* 125-150.

Pressley, M. (1995). *Cognitive strategy instruction that really improves children's academic performance* (2nd ed.). Cambridge, MA: Brookline Books.

Pressley, M., El-Dinary, P.B., & Brown, R. (1992). Skilled and not-so-skilled reading: Good information processing and not-so-good information processing. In M. Pressley, K.R. Harris, & J.R. Guthrie (Eds.), *Promoting academic competence and literacy in school* (pp. 91-127). San Diego: Academic Press.

Pressley, M., Ghetala, E.S., Woloshyn, V., & Pirie, J. (1990). Sometimes adults miss the main ideas and do not realize it: Confidence in response to short-answer and multiple-choice comprehension questions. *Reading Research Quarterly, 25,* 232-249.

Pressley, M., Symons, S., McDaniel, M.A., Snyder, B.L., & Turner, J.E. (1988). Elaborative interrogation facilities in the acquisition of confusing facts. *Journal of Educational Psychology, 80,* 301-342.

Pressley, M., Wood, E., Woloshyn, V.E., Martin, V., King, A., & Menk, D. (1992). Encouraging mindful use of prior knowledge: Attempting to construct explanatory answers facilitates learning. *Educational Psychologist, 27,*

91-110.

Putnam, R.T. (1987). Structuring and adjusting content for students: A study of live and simulated tutoring of addition. *American Educational Research Journal, 24*, 13-48.

Reiser, B.J., Connelly, J.W., Ranney, M., & Ritter, C. (1992). *The role of explanatory feedback in skill acquisition.* Unpublished manuscript, Princeton University, Princeton, NJ.

Rogoff, B. (1990).*Apprenticeship in thinking.* New York: Oxford University Press.

Roschelle, J. (1992). Learning by collaboration: Convergent conceptual change. *The Journal of the Learning Sciences, 2*, 235-276.

Scardamalia, M., & Bereiter, C. (1991). Higher levels of agency for children in knowledge building: A challenge for the design of new knowledge media. *The Journal of the Learning Sciences, 1*, 37-68.

Schofield, J.W., Eurich-Fulcer, R., & Britt, C.L. (1994). Teachers, computer tutors, and teaching: The artificially intelligent tutor as an agent for classroom change. *American Educational Research Journal, 31*, 579-607.

Schwartz, D.L. (1995). The emergence of abstract representations in dyad problem solving. *The Journal of the Learning Sciences, 4*, 321-354.

Sinclair, J.M., & Coulthart, R. M. (1975). *Toward an analysis of discourse.* New York: Oxford University Press.

Slavin, R.E. (1983). When does cooperative learning increase student achievement? *Psychological Bulletin, 94*, 429-445.

Smith, V.L., & Clark, H.H. (1993). On the course of answering questions. *Journal of Memory and Language, 32*, 25-38.

Stevens, A., Collins, A., & Goldin, S.E. (1982). Misconceptions in students' understanding. In D. Sleeman & J.S. Brown (Eds.), *Intelligent tutoring systems* (pp. 13-24). New York: Academic Press.

Sweller, J. (1988). Cognitive load during problem solving: Effects on learning. *Cognitive Science, 12*, 257-285.

Trabasso, T., & Suh, S.Y. (1993). Using talk-aloud protocols to reveal inferences during comprehension of text. *Discourse Processes, 16*, 3-34.

VanLehn, K. (1990). Mind bugs: The origins of procedural misconceptions. Cambridge, MA: MIT Press.

VanLehn, K., Jones, R.M., & Chi, M.T.H. (1992). A model of the self-explanation effect. *The Journal of the Learning Sciences, 2*, 1-59.

Weaver, C., & Bryant, D. (1995). Monitoring of comprehension: The role of text difficulty in metamemory for narrative and expository text. *Memory and Cognition, 23*, 12-22.

Webb, N.B. (1989). Peer interaction and learning in small groups. *International Journal of Educational Research, 13*, 21-40.

Webb, N.M., Troper, J.D., & Fall, R. (1995). Constructive activity and learning in collaborative small groups. *Journal of Educational Psychology, 87,* 406-423.

Wittrock, M.C. (1990). Generative processes of comprehension. *Educational Psychologist, 24,* 345-376.

Zimmerman, B.J., Bandura, A., & Martinez-Pons, M. (1992). Self-motivation for academic attainment: The role of self-efficacy beliefs and personal goal setting. *American Educational Research Journal, 29,* 663-676.

Becoming a Scaffolder of Students' Learning

KATHLEEN HOGAN & MICHAEL PRESSLEY,
The University at Albany, State University of New York

The five chapters in this book present many tips for effectively scaffolding student learning. In addition to analyzing the mechanics of scaffolding, the authors also considered the subtler dimensions of using scaffolding competently. A repertoire of techniques, a deep knowledge of the subject matter, and a constructivist philosophy go a long way toward supporting successful implementation of scaffolding.

Although lists of teaching tactics cannot prescribe a teacher's personal style and adaptations to different groups of students, the following are presented as general guidelines for getting started using scaffolding as part of your instructional repertoire. As is noted in Chapter 4, even though a good scaffolder must be sensitive to each individual student, there are many general goals and strategies that can guide all scaffolding interactions.

The following lists organize the chapters' recommendations about scaffolding within three time frames: things to do before scaffolding, during scaffolding, and while maintaining scaffolding as a pervasive part of your classroom practice.

1. PREPARING TO USE SCAFFOLDING AS AN INSTRUCTIONAL TECHNIQUE

- **Examine whether and how scaffolding complements your personal goals as a teacher.** Scaffolding needs to make sense within the larger framework of your teaching, so it is helpful to articulate to yourself the role you would like scaffolding to play in your teaching. For example, for many teachers, scaffolding makes sense as students try to use competencies they have just learned.

- **Listen to your current classroom dialogue.** Decide what is productive and counterproductive about the verbal interactions in your classroom. Eliminate counterproductive interchanges such as corrections that come across as unintended criticisms of students. Does the responsibility for thinking lie with the students, or do you lead them with questions that test recall more than thinking? Do students spur one another's thinking through questions and comments? Plan to build your scaffolding practice from a foundation of strong interactions that already exist, and to use scaffolding to modify weaker modes of interaction.

- **Decide what to scaffold.** Scaffolding can be used to promote students' knowledge of content, their use of cognitive and metacognitive strategies, or the development of their personal styles and dispositions. Although a number of these areas might be touched upon in a given scaffolding sequence, it is helpful to have a primary goal in mind for each interaction.

- **Plan a macrostructure for scaffolding.** For instance, you might decide on a general structure for progressively increasing demands on students' thinking. If you want your students to learn and use complex strategies, think about how, over time, the use of such strategies can be introduced and their application scaffolded.

- **Plan to match different scaffolding techniques to different contexts.** Consider whether you will have an opportunity to scaffold individuals, small groups, and/or the whole class during a given class period. Think through which types of scaffolding goals require intensive one-to-one work, and which can be accomplished effectively with a higher student-to-scaffolder ratio. Consider how scaffolding techniques need to be altered for these different settings.

- **Set motivational as well as instructional goals.** Effective scaffolders set out to promote students' curiosity, self-esteem, self-confidence, self-efficacy, and the like. Keep in mind the potential affective benefits of scaffolding so that you can make plans to maximize this potential.
- **Choose to scaffold topics and strategies that you know well.** Background knowledge in a discipline, as well as knowledge about typical student difficulties and effective ways of dealing with them, are all crucial to effective scaffolding. Therefore, choose an area in which you are well versed to begin practicing scaffolding techniques.

2. USING SCAFFOLDING AS A TOOL FOR CLASSROOM INSTRUCTION

- **Recruit students' interest and establish a shared goal.** For scaffolding to be most effective, students should be motivated to achieve an endpoint that you and they envision together (e.g., understanding ecological relationships in their neighborhood, or publishing a book of the students' stories). Clarifying the desired goal is a crucial first step in scaffolding.
- **Maintain the pursuit of goals.** This is accomplished in part by controlling for frustration and discouragement, which can derail students' motivation to keep on trying. Part of scaffolding is finding a simpler version of a task if students are experiencing great difficulty with an initial assignment.
- **Use a Socratic style of interaction** that includes asking lots of higher-order questions to prompt deep reasoning rather than

recitation. These include "What if..." questions, such as "What if an insecticide wiped out all of the insects in the neighborhood? What would be the effect on the local ecology?"

- **Continuously remain aware of your students' cognitive and affective states and their levels of competence.** Keep the tasks a little bit challenging —not too easy, and not too hard. Easy tasks bore, and overly hard ones frustrate. Tasks that are just right motivate and engage students by making it seem possible for them to make progress with some effort.
- **Provide feedback, but avoid directly evaluating students' thinking.** Encourage students to decide for themselves whether they are making progress, and if they are not, to think about another approach. Being indirect, such as implying that something is wrong or right, will encourage students to judge their own work and help them internalize performance standards.
- **Model thinking processes.** Making your own thinking visible is an excellent way to communicate desired thinking strategies and dispositions to students.
- **Coach and assist students' practice.** For instance, you might direct students' attention to important features of problems as they work.
- **Provide tailored assistance.** This is accomplished by adapting your level of assistance to the level of a student's needs.
- **Provide explanations as necessary.** Direct instruction can be useful during scaffolding—for instance, to initiate the development of a new skill.
- **Encourage and capitalize on students' comments and questions.** Make sure, however, that you understand their questions before responding to them. In whole-class settings, help the rest of the class understand a student's question. An effective scaffolder takes student questions seriously and uses them as material for moving students' thinking along.
- **Be patient while collaborating with students to produce**

answers. This means resisting the temptation to fill in the gaps in their thinking. Instead, use "pumps" and "prompts" to encourage students to keep thinking aloud. Then allow them to summarize for themselves what has been learned.

- **Show a high level of affective support and nurturance.** Give polite but accurate feedback on mistakes, and attribute failure to problem difficulty. Do all that you can to minimize students' failure and maximize their success.

- **Respond flexibly to students' errors.** There are a range of tactics for responding to errors, including ignoring, forestalling, or debugging them, or intervening to make corrections. The context and goals will determine which response is most appropriate.

- **Fade the intensity of your support** as you release responsibility for determining the next steps to the learners. Prompt reflection for internalization and generalization.

3. SUSTAINING A CULTURE OF THOUGHTFULNESS

- **Maintain an atmosphere that supports intellectual risk-taking.** The social fabric of the classroom can itself become a kind of scaffold, especially when modeled after the social norms of the discipline being studied. Gradully a culture of thinking together with students will develop, and students will take on more responsibility for maintaining that culture.

- **Be explicit about how and why you are scaffolding.** Students should understand the rules of intellectual support and collaboration so they can become master players of the game. The more you make your scaffolding style transparent, the more you empower students to make the scaffolding partnership successful.

- **Keep weighing the benefits and costs of scaffolding.** Scaffolding instruction will not be the most efficient or effective means of meeting every instruction goal. Also, it is an exhausting way to teach, so it cannot be sustained all day, every day. Therefore, you'll have to be selective and target your use of scaffolding to those areas where it is likely to do the job better than any other technique.

SUMMARY

The chapters in this book illustrate many kinds of scaffolding techniques. But are there any elements that are common to all of the examples? When can we label a teaching approach *scaffolding* instead of some other pedagogical term, such as *strategy instruction* or *responsive teaching?* We suggest that on-line diagnosis of students' needs is a defining element of scaffolding. As a teacher scaffolds, she or he determines the amount of support required for the learner to make and sustain progress, thereby discovering the student's level of competence. So scaffolding is a form of dynamic assessment as well as a form of instruction. It is also a tool for instructional decision making, as diagnosis provides guidance about what instruction needs to occur next.

Defining scaffolding as including active diagnosis means that the effective unskilled tutors described in Chapter 5, who do not make sophisticated diagnoses of students' needs and prior knowledge, could be characterized as *assisting* learning, rather than as *scaffolding*. The analysis of these tutors suggests that peers who are not sophisticated enough to diagnose a classmate's understanding—and are thus technically unable to scaffold—might nonetheless be effective tutors.

Two other essential elements of scaffolding are a commitment to letting students do the thinking, or to collaborating as a partner in students' thinking, and a gradual removal of the support. Different kinds of learners need more or less sturdy scaffolding for greater or lesser amounts of time, so internalization of the scaffolded knowledge, skills, and dispositions will proceed at varying rates for different students.

PARTING THOUGHTS

One beneficial outcome of incorporating scaffolding into your daily practice will be your own professional growth. You will learn as you scaffold. Your knowlege and understanding will grow as you do the hard thinking about tasks and students that scaffolding requires. You will acquire a deeper understanding of the content and processes within the knowledge domain you are teaching, and gain new insights about your students as learners. Also, your sense of yourself as an effective teacher promoting students' learning will surely grow as you observe the results of your scaffolding.

Expertise is developed through experience, and experience is gained through practice. Because scaffolding is an effortful process that is full of challenges, it will take time to master. Yet if unskilled tutors can be effective, then certainly a skilled teacher who is just learning how to scaffold can promote learning gains. Thus, your students only stand to benefit from your learning process.

Finally, remember that scaffolding is not a stand-alone approach to instruction, but one element within the philosophy and techniques that guide your teaching. The teachers whose practices were examined in the preceding chapters have incorporated scaffolding not just into their bank of skills, but also into their personal philosophies about their roles as teachers and students' roles as learners. Their stories provide heartening indications that those who rise to the challenge of effective instruction through scaffolding present models of exemplary practice, from which we can learn and draw inspiration. We hope that you, too, will find a place for scaffolding techniques in your personal teaching repertoire.

Index

A

American Association for the Advancement of Science, 98

Anderson, J.R., Corbett, A.T., Koedinger, K.R., & Pelletier, R., 146, 184, 153, 156, 160

Applebee, A.N. & Langer, J.A., 82

Argyris, C., 44

Astington, J.W., & Olson, D.R., 85

B

Beed, P.L., Hawkins, E.M., & Roller, C.M., 46

Bereiter, C., & Scardamalia, M., 153

Benchmark School, 3, 47, 48, 49, 50, 63, 66

Berk, L.E., & Winsler, A., 110, 121

Bloom, B.S., 109, 146

Brammer, L.M., & Shostrom, E.L., 102

Bransford, J.D., Franks, J.J., Vye, N.J., & Sherwood, R.D., 153

Bransford, J.D., Goldman, S.R., & Vye, N.J., 157, 166

Brown, A.L., 79, 84, 152, 166

Brown, A.L., Bransford, J.D., Ferrara, R.A., & Campione, J.C., 153

Brown, J.S., Collins, A. & Dugiud, P., 47

Bruner, J., 9, 89, 152

Burns-Hoffman, R., 82

C

Cawsey, A., 165

Chabay, R.W., & Sherwood, B.A., 122

Chi, M.T., Bassock, M., Lewis, M.W., Reimann, P., & Glaser, R., 154, 163

Chi, M.T.H., deLeeuw, N., Chiu, M-H., & LaVancher, C., 137, 163

Clark, H.H., & Schaefer, E.F., 153, 168, 170

Clay, M.M., 140

Cobb, P., 79

Cobb, P., Wood, T., & Yackel, E., 89, 104

Cohen, P.A., Kulik, J.A., & Kulik, C.C., 146

Collier, J.L., & Collier, C., 53

Collins, A., Brown, J.S., & Newman, S.E., 158

Collins, A., & Stevens, A.L., 109, 133

content knowledge, 50
  recognizing, building patterns, 50
  strategies, 55

Cordova, D.I., & Lepper, M.R., 127

D

Dahlgren, K., 170

data collection & analysis, 15
  qualitative methods, 15
    constant comparative, 15
    stages of, 16

Day, J.D., & Cordon, L.A., 81, 82, 87

Dede, C.J., 126

delayed readers, 43, 47

Derry, S.J., 127

Derry, S. J., Hawkes, L.W., & Tsai, C., 127

dialogue, 74

key to cognitive growth, 74

verbal scaffolding, 74

Diaz, R.M., Neal, C.J., & Vachio, A., 77

Dillon, J.T., 164

DiPardo, A., & Freedman, S., 10

discussion, elements of, 66

Doyle, W., 9

Driver, L., Asoko, H., Leach, J., Mortimer, E., & Scott, P., 79

Duell, O.K., 167

Duffy, G., & Roehler, L., 14

Duffy, G., Roehler, L., & Herrmann, B., 20, 48

Duffy, G., Roehler, L., Meloth, M., & Vavrus, L., 17

Duffy, G., Roehler, L., & Rackliffe, G., 10

Dweck, C.S., 132, 136

Dweck, C.S., & Leggett, E.L., 132

E

English as a Second Language (ESL), 12

learning environment of classroom, 13

F

Fenstermaker, G., 38

Ferrara, K., 171

Fitz-Gibbon, C.R., 146

Flavell, J.H., Miller, P.H., & Miller, S.M., 86

Foersterling, F., 136

Foos, P.W., Mora, J.J., & Tkacz, S., 137

Forbes, E., 53

Fox, B., 151, 156, 169

G

Gagne, R.M., 158

Gallas, K., 104

Gallimore, R., & Tharp, R., 10, 11, 37

Gardner, H., 43

Gaskins, I.W., Anderson, R.C., Pressley, M., Cunicelli, E.A., & Satlow, E., 47

Gaskins, I.W., & Elliot, T.T., 48

Gavelek, J., 8

Glaser, B., 15

Glaser, B., & Strauss, A., 15

Glenberg, A.M., Wilkinson, A.C., & Epstein, W., 154

Goldman, S.R., Pelligrino, J.W., & Bransford, J.D., 157

Goldenberg, C., 10

Goleman, D., 44

Gorden, R., 15

Graesser, A.C., & Person, N.K., 146, 149, 163, 164, 167

Graesser, A.C., Person, N.K., Magliano, J.P., 149, 152, 155, 158, 160, 164, 166, 167, 171, 172, 175

Graesser, A.C., Singer, M., & Trabasso, T., 163

guidelines for use of scaffolding, 186

as culture of thoughtfulness, 189

as instructional technique, 186

as tool for classroom, 187

H

Hall, E.A., 77

Hatabo, G., 78, 79

Hogan, K., Pressley, M., & Nastasi, B.K., 75

Hume, G.P., Michael, J.A., Rovick, A., & Evens, M.W., 172

Hunt, D., 102

I

INSPIRE, (Intelligent, Nurturant, Socratic, Progressively demanding, Indirect, Reflective, Encouraging), 4, 129, 130

J

Johnson & Johnson, 166

K

Keats, E.J., 33
Kellogg, S., 35
Kerr, T., 164
King, A., 85, 153, 166
Kleifgen, J.A., 81

L

Lajoie, S.P., & Derry, S.J., 140
Lampert, M., 10
Langer, J.A., 82, 97
language arts, parts of, 68
 discussion, reading, writing, 68
Larkin, J.H., & Chabay, R.W., 126, 140
learning principles, 37
 balance of challenge & support, 37
 collaboration, 39
 manner, 38
 need to embrace complexity, 38
 question & comment, 38
LeFevre, J.A., & Dixon, P. 160
Leinhardt, G., 121
Leonte'ev, A.N., 88
Lepper, M.R., Aspinwall, L.G., Mumme, D.L., Chabay, R.W., 77, 80, 121, 136, 138, 151, 155, 164
Lepper, M.R. & Chabay, R.W., 122, 140
Lepper, M.R., & Malone, T.W., 138
Lepper, M.R., Woolverton, M., Mumme, D.L., & Guntis, J.L., 156

Lesgold, A., Lajoie, S., Bunzo, M., & Eggan, G., 148, 156, 160
Levine, H.M., Glass, E., & Meister, G., 140

M

Madden, N., Slavin, R., Karweit, N., Dolan, L., & Wosik, B., 166
Malone, T.W., & Lepper, M.R., 138
Martin, J., 10
mathematical thinking, 63
McArthur, D., Stacz, C., Zmuidzinas, M., 77, 80, 151, 156, 162, 172
Mehan, H., 167
Merrill, D.C., Reiser, B.J., Merrill, S.K., & Landes, S., 122
Merrill, D.C., Reiser, B.J., Ranney, M., & Trafton, J.G., 151, 172
Mohan, M., 146
Moll, L.A., & Whitmore, K.F., 78
Moore, J.D., 165
Musser, G., & Burger, W., 32

N

National Research Council, 98
Nelson, K.E., 137
Newman, D., Griffin, P., & Cole, M., 78
Newman, R.S., & Goldin, L., 84

O

O'Connor, M.C., & Michaels, S., 104
Office of Naval Research project, 148
 naturalistic tutoring, samples of, 148, 149
 critical points, 149-150
Ohlsson, S., 153
one-to-one tutoring, 77, 78, 88, 109
 difficulties for classroom teachers, 88
 Plato, Aristotle, Socrates, 108

P

Palincsar, A., Anderson, C., &
     David, Y., 10
Palincsar, A.S., & Brown, A., 153,
     158
Papert, S., 152
Paris, C., 165
Paris, S., Lipson, M., & Wixson, K.,
     17
Parker, L.E., & Lepper, M.R., 127
Pearson, P.D., 10
Pearson, P.D., & Fielding, L., 45
Perkins, D., 43, 49, 84
Person, N.K., 149, 154, 157, 158,
     159, 161, 162, 166, 171, 172
Person, N.K., Graesser, A.C.,
     Magliano, J.P., & Kreuz, R.J.,
     149, 155
Person, N.K., Kreuz, R.J., Zwaan,
     R., & Graesser, A.C., 149, 154,
     155, 170
Piagetian theory, 78
Pinchot, G., & Pinchot, E., 45
Polya, G., 63, 141
Poole, D., 153
Pratt, M.W., Green, D., MacVicar,
     J., & Boutrogianni, M., 77,
Pressley, M., 153
Pressley, M., El-Dinary., P.B., &
     Brown, R., 153
Pressley, M., El-Dinary, P.B.,
     Gaskins, I.W., Schuder, T.,
     Bergman, J.L., Almasi, J., &
     Brown, R., 47
Pressley, M., Ghetala, E.S.,
     Woloshyn, V., & Pirie, J., 153
Pressley, M., Hogan, K., Wharton-
     McDonald, R., Mistretta, J., &
     Ettenberger, S., 77, 86, 96
Pressley, M., Symons, S., McDaniel,
     M.A., Snyder, B.L., & Turner,
     J.E., 163
Pressley, M., Wood, E., Woloshyn,
     V.E., Martin, V., King, A., &
     Menk, D., 163

Putnam, R.T., 151, 156, 162

R

Raphael, T., Goatley, V., McMahon,
     S., & Woodman, D., 14
reading assignments, 53
     My Brother Sam Is Dead, 53
     Johnny Tremain, 53
Reif, F., & Larkin, J.H., 79
Reiser, B.J., Connelly, J.W., Ranney,
     M., & Ritter, C., 156
responsive teaching, language of, 89
Roehler, L., & Duffy, G., 17, 20
Roehler, L., Hallenback, M.,
     McLellan, M., & Svoboda, N.,
     11
Rogoff, B., 45, 47, 78, 158, 166
Rommetveit, R., 9
Roschelle, J., 153

S

San Souci, R.D., & Pinckney, B., 30
scaffolding, 11
     characteristics of, 11
     data collection & analysis,, 15
     social constructivist approach to,
          12, 37
     types of, 7, 11, 16
scaffolding, community approach to,
     99
     flexibility, 99
     students' perspectives, 100
scaffolding, definition of, 45
scaffolding, developing skills in, 102-
     103
     future research on, 103
scaffolding, guiding questions, role
     of, 7
scaffolding in action, 49
     assisted performance by teachers,
          50
scaffolding, instructional, 75, 79
     characteristics of, 82, 83-84

community of inquiry, 88
control from teacher to student, 82
large-class settings, difficulties, 84,
  85, 86, 87
unifying framework, 102
zone of proximal development
  (ZPD), 77
scaffolding, meaning of, 2
component of teaching activity, 9
role of, 7
characteristics, 7, 11
types of, 7, 11
scaffolding, requirements of, 9
conversations, types of, 10
  instructional, 2, 10
  learning, 11
intersubjectivity, 9
scaffolding, supportive situations, 71
scaffolding, types of, 16, 17
explanations, 17
  conditional/situational knowl-
    edge, 17
  declarative/prepositional
    knowledge, 17
  procedural knowledge, 17
student participation in, 18
verifying/clarifying understanding,
  18
Scardamalia, M., & Bereiter, C., 152
Schofield, J.W., Eurich-Fulcer, R, &
  Britt, C.L., 147
Schwartz, D.L., 166
science education, standards, 98
motivation to learn, 98
search process, as element of research
  plan, 59
e.g., understanding weather, 59
Searles, D., 82, 86
Seligman, M.E.P., 44
Semb, G.B., Ellis, J.A., & Aranjo, J.,
  85
Senge, P.M., 45
Shulman, L.S., 87, 130

Sinclair, J.M., & Coulthart, R.M.,
  167
Slavin, R.E., 166
Sleeman, D., & Brown, J.S., 126
Sleeman, D., Kelly, A.E., Martinak,
  R., Ward, R.D., & Moore, J.S.,
  126
Smagorinsky, P., 8
Smith, V.L., & Clark, H.H., 169
social constructivist model, 8, 12
use of, 11
zone of proximal development
  (ZPD), definition of, 8, 9
social nature of classrooms, 1
dialogue, 1
instructional scaffolding, 1, 2
Steele, C.M., 139
Steele, C.M., & Aronson, J., 139
Sternberg, R. J., 38, 43
Stevens, A.L., Collins, A., & Goldin,
  S.E., 110, 133, 158
Stone, C.A., 77, 78, 80, 81
suggestions for teachers, 177-179
Sweller, J., 160

T
teaching and learning, description of,
  14
Book Club format, 14
  Author's Chair, 15
  editing area, 14
  sharing area, 14
literacy cycles, 14, 15
Tharp, R.G. & Gallimore, R., 45,
  47, 50, 82, 84, 89
Trabasso, T., & Suh, S.Y., 163
transactional strategies instruction,
  47, 48
for delayed readers, 47
tutoring, 112
mathematics as subject matter, 112
procedure for sessions, 113
selection criteria of tutees, 113

tutoring, computer-based, 147, 148
  curriculum scripts, use of, 162
  "prompting," use of, 170
  "pumping," use of, 169
  splicing, 171
tutoring, criteria for improvement, 114
  cognitive and/or affective gains, 114
tutoring, "gold standard" of education, 109
tutoring, naturalistic, 145
  components of, 147
    absence of, 151
    curriculum scripts, use of, 162, 176
    dialogue between tutor & student, effectiveness of, 166
    error diagnosis, 156
    explanatory reasoning, 163
      prevalence of, 164
    "hinting," 172, 173
    macro- and microanalyses, 150
      prevalence of, 159
    question-answering frame, 167
    prompting by tutor, 170
    pumping by tutor, 168
    splicing, 171
    shared meanings, 153
      feedback, flaws in, 154, 155, 156
    Socratic method, nonexistent, 158
tutoring, nonprofessional, 140
  computer-based, 140
  paraprofessional volunteer, 140
  parental, 140
  peer tutoring programs, 140
tutoring, unskilled, 146
  effectiveness of, 146
tutors, motivation goals, 126
  challenge, 126
  confidence, 126

  control, 127
  curiosity, 127
  decisions, importance of, 127
  indirect strategy, 136
  self-confidence
    cultivation of, 127
    promotion of 138
tutors, responses to student errors, 122, 128
  debugging, 124
  forestalling, 122
  indirect style, 135
  ignoring, 122
  intervening, 123
tutors, expert
  identification of, 115
  effectiveness of, 115, 116
  structure of sessions, 120
    problem selection/presentation, 120-121
    problem solution, 121
tutors, scaffolding techniques of, 108
tutors, successful, 129
  commitment to progress, 134
  enthusiasm of, 132
  inspiring learning, 129, 130
  intelligence, knowledge of, 130
    subject-specific, 131
  reflection, 136
  sensitive to emotions of tutees, 132
  Socratic style, 133
    encouraging curiosity, 138

V
VanLehn, K., 148, 160
VanLehn, K., Jones, R.M., & Chi, M.T.H., 158
Venn diagram, 32
von Glasersfeld, E., 99
Vygotskian & Piagetian theories, 78, 79
social constructivism, 79

Vygotsky, L.S., 8, 45, 77, 78, 121

W

Waitley, D., 45
Weaver, C. & Bryant, D., 154
Webb, N.B., 163
Webb, N.M., Troper, J.D., & Fall, R., 163
Wenger, E., 126
Wertsch, J., 8, 89, 121
Wertsch, J., McNamee, G., McLare, J., & Budwig, N., 8
Wick, C.W. & Leon, L.S., 45
Wittrock, M.C., 152
Wong, S., 82
Wood, D., Bruner, J., & Ross, G., 9, 45, 77, 78, 82, 110

Wood, D.J., Hood, H.A., & Middleton, D.J., 110
Wood, D.J., & Middleton, D.J., 110, 134

Z

Zimmerman, B.J., Bandura, A., & Martinez-Pons, M., 152
zone of proximal development (ZPD), 8, 9, 11, 45, 46, 77, 81
  assisted modeling, 46
  assisted performance, 45, 48
  cognitive apprenticeship, 47
  element identification, 46
  responsive teaching, 47
  strategy naming, 46

About the Editors

Kathleen Hogan is Educational Research & Development Specialist at the Institute of Ecosystem Studies in Millbrook, NY, and a doctoral candidate in educational psychology and statistics at the University of Albany, State University of New York. Her research focuses on students' cognition during scientific inquiry, particularly on the actual and potential roles of cognitive strategies and metacognition during inquiry, and on peers and the teacher as students' partners in knowledge construction. She is the author of several research articles and three books: *Eco-Inquiry: A guide to ecological learning experiences for the upper elementary/middle grades; Rita,* a novel about thinking for ages 9–12; and *Promoting student thinking: A guide to linking science and literature through Rita.*

Michael Pressley, Ph.D., is Professor in the Department of Educational Psychology at the University of Albany, State University of New York. He has studied student cognition, especially students' use of strategies, for about 20 years, including programs of research on children's imagery, mnemonics, cognitive monitoring, and reading comprehension. He is the author or co-author of more than 200 scientific publications and is considered an expert in the areas of children's memory, educational psychology, and reading comprehension. In addition to the present volume, Mr. Pressley has recently co-authored five books: doctoral, intermediate, and undergraduate level textbooks in educational psychology, all from HarperCollins; *Verbal Protocols of Reading: The Nature of Constructively Responsive Reading,* published by Erlbaum and Associates; and the best-selling textbook *Cognitive Strategy Instruction that Really Improves Children's Academic Performance,* from Brookline Books.